True Tales of

LIFE & DEATH AT FORT ADAMS

TRUE TALES OF

LIFE & DEATH AT FORT ADAMS

KATHLEEN TROOST-CRAMER

FOREWORD BY
ROBERT J. McCORMACK
THE FORT ADAMS TRUST

Published by The History Press
Charleston, SC 29403
www.historypress.net

Copyright © 2013 by Kathleen Troost-Cramer
All rights reserved

Cover: Fort images taken by the author. Vintage images of soldiers appear courtesy of the Fort Adams Trust.

Unless otherwise noted, images appear courtesy of the author.

First published 2013
Second printing 2014

Manufactured in the United States

ISBN 978.1.62619.108.2

Library of Congress Cataloging-in-Publication Data

Troost-Cramer, Kathleen.
True tales of life and death at Fort Adams / Kathleen Troost-Cramer.
pages cm. -- (Landmarks)
Summary: "This book chronicles the lives and deaths of people living at Fort Adams in Newport, Rhode Island"-- Provided by publisher.
ISBN 978-1-62619-108-2 (pbk.)
1. Fort Adams (Newport, R.I.) 2. Fort Adams (Newport, R.I.)--Biography. 3. Newport (R.I.)--History. 4. Newport (R.I.)--Biography. I. Title.
F89.N5T76 2013
974.5'7--dc23
2013022222

Notice: The information in this book is true and complete to the best of our knowledge. It is offered without guarantee on the part of the author or The History Press. The author and The History Press disclaim all liability in connection with the use of this book.

All rights reserved. No part of this book may be reproduced or transmitted in any form whatsoever without prior written permission from the publisher except in the case of brief quotations embodied in critical articles and reviews.

To my parents, Donna and Hans.
Took me long enough, huh?

CONTENTS

Foreword, by Robert J. McCormack 9
Acknowledgements 11

1. Madness and Bloodshed 13
2. "Hurried into Eternity": Death from the Deep 39
3. Accidental Death 57
4. The Grip of Death's Hand: Influenza, 1918 73
5. Cold Case: The Strange Demise of Mary Gleason 81
6. Do They Still Stand Watch? Reports of Strange Phenomena at Fort Adams 91

Appendix: Chronological Listing of Death Events at Fort Adams 103
Notes 105
Bibliography 119
Index 135
About the Author 139

Foreword

Visitors approaching the main gates of Fort Adams cannot help being struck by the sheer size and scale of this massive fortress. You need not even enter to be impressed by its looming exterior walls, behind which once lay the most complex defenses ever constructed by the military of the United States.

It is unfortunate that this fortress, which proudly guarded Narragansett Bay and Newport Harbor for generations, has fallen into disrepair. While no enemy ever took the fort, wind, weather and vegetation have inflicted tremendous damage.

Although great progress has been made in recent years to reclaim this fortress from the elements, as of today, Fort Adams has yet to regain all its former glory. As a result, it's difficult for today's visitors to imagine this National Historic Landmark as it once was: home to a bustling community of soldiers and their families.

The stories Kathleen tells in her book bring Fort Adams back to life. Once again you can experience the sights and sounds of people leading their daily lives within the walls of North America's largest coastal fortification. While her stories focus primarily on how people met their end, you'll also find stories of hope and inspiration.

I found one such story of hope in Kathleen's tale of the Henry family in the chapter "Madness and Bloodshed." The way she described the Fort Adams community coming together to aid the family in the face of such tragedy was inspiring. I was similarly moved by the valor and humanitarian effort of the men of Fort Adams, Goat Island and the City of Newport as they came together to help their fellow countrymen in the struggle for their lives described in chapter 3.

Through extensive research, Kathleen brings vivid detail to stories that many familiar with Fort Adams knew as little more than rumor or folklore. Her storytelling ability combined with a detailed investigation into facts and circumstances allows you to engage in the events that took place here and to draw your own conclusions.

I'm sure you'll enjoy the stories Kathleen tells in *True Tales of Life and Death at Fort Adams*. If you purchased your copy in the Fort Adams Gift Shop, on behalf of the Fort Adams Trust, I thank you for your support. If not, I hope these stories inspire you to visit our beautiful corner of the world, this waterfront fortress once home to generations of workers, soldiers and their families.

Robert J. McCormack, Director of Marketing and the Visitor Experience
The Fort Adams Trust
Newport, Rhode Island
May 2013

Acknowledgements

This book rides the coattails of giants. I could never have brought these stories together had it not been for those who did painstaking research before me. My thanks to Father Robert Hayman, whose transcriptions of old *Newport Mercury* articles provided a springboard for my research, and to Vin Arnold, who was responsible for the passing on of this information to the Fort Adams Trust. Thanks to my friend and fellow Fort Adams tour guide John T. Duchesneau, whose online history of Fort Adams, collection of images and personal knowledge were not only invaluable but also great fun to acquire; and to Professor Daniel P. Titus of Salve Regina University, without whose cemetery study, collections of clippings and images and kind help and enthusiasm for this project, this book would be a short story. I could never have done this without all of you.

To my family, who now know what it's like to live with a writer—thank you for putting up with my obsessions with all these stories and for the beyond-the-call sacrifices of time you've all made to help me make this happen. The end result is just as much the product of your hard work as it is of mine.

Thanks to everyone at The History Press, especially Jeff, Alyssa and Darcy, who took a chance on this book and on this previously unpublished writer. Because of your faith in this project, a lifelong dream has come true.

Thanks to those research professionals who gave their best efforts to help me tie up loose ends: Ken Carlson at the Rhode Island State Archives and Nathaniel Wiltzen at the National Archives in Boston, both of whom separately shared my frustration at the lack of available records for events at Fort Adams; Andy at the Rhode Island Judicial Archives, who spent hours trying to discover the fate of Corporal Nicholson on my behalf; and Jim, Phoebe, Dana and all the staff at the Rhode Island Historical Society Library, without whose assistance I would never have discovered the result of Nicholson's case or the story behind the Geary baby's headstone in the fort cemetery.

Thanks to Rob, Laurie, Nagele and all the employees and volunteers of the Fort Adams Trust, who every day engage tirelessly in efforts to preserve and maintain this endangered National Historic Landmark and to educate others about it. Thanks for letting me surf the archives and wander about the fort on my own taking pictures; and most of all, thanks for giving me the opportunity to guide others around this very special place. *You* are "the Rock on Which the Storm Will Beat."

And to Erik—thanks for helping this tech-challenged author sort out the differences between dpi, pixels and everything in between. And in response to your last Facebook message—we all miss you, too.

Chapter 1

Madness and Bloodshed

The LORD asked Cain, "Where is your brother?" Cain answered, "I don't know. Am I my brother's keeper?" Then the LORD said…"Your brother's blood cries out to me from the ground!"
—Genesis 4:9–10 (NAB)

First Blood

The midsummer night was warm and still. The watch on duty had been uneventful. It was July 4—the precise twentieth anniversary of the commissioning of Fort Adams, the artillery base that guarded the entrance to the harbor at Newport, Rhode Island. Newport well remembered the scars the British forces had left during the Revolution and had replaced the old Revolutionary earthworks battery with the brick Fort Adams, designed by top French engineer Major Louis Tousard and housing seventeen cannon, to ensure that the city would never see such an invasion again. Above the gate, a sign proclaimed that this state-of-the-art artillery emplacement was "The Rock on Which the Storm Will Beat."

Back then, no one could have foreseen the storm that would break twenty years later, when this place of safety would see its first act of deliberate violence—from two men both dedicated to the same cause, wearing the same uniform, who ought to have been comrades in arms but proved more deadly to each other than any foreign enemy.

Fort Adams in 1819, the year William Cornell murdered William Kane. *National Archives; compiled by Bolling W. Smith and acquired courtesy of John T. Duchesneau.*

Young Private William G. Cornell, along with a fellow soldier, had just finished his turn at guard duty on the night of Fort Adams' twentieth birthday, July 4, 1819, at about ten o'clock. As protocol dictated, after the relief guard arrived, the two men were escorted back to their barracks by a corporal on duty, shouldering their loaded muskets. As the trio passed along the rows of doorways to the barracks, Cornell's eye caught the figure of nineteen-year-old Private William Kane lounging in a doorway.

As Cornell approached, the air must have thickened with tension. There was bad blood between him and Kane. To the present day, no one knows the cause of their hostilities. What is known is that about two weeks previously, the men had had some argument during which Cornell, "in a high passion," promised to kill Kane at the earliest opportunity—apparently with little

Fort Adams' six-and-a-half-acre parade field today. The much smaller 1799 fort was situated within this area.

sense that his words would be remembered and taken seriously. Cornell's threat was surprising, given that "the parties…were good friends afterwards, living in the same quarters."[1]

But if Cornell still harbored rage against Kane on that July 4 night, he bit it back. He strode by without incident, stoically staring ahead, not even glancing in Kane's direction—perhaps clenching his jaw with every step.

As Cornell passed, Kane laughed quietly.

Still, Cornell held himself in check, swallowing his anger, marching behind the corporal escort alongside his fellow soldier.

Then Kane did something completely inexplicable. Forgetting—or disregarding—Cornell's previous threat against his life, Kane stepped out of the doorway, bent down, picked up a handful of little gravel pebbles and casually chucked them at Cornell's back, as if he deliberately meant to needle the man.

Now provoked beyond endurance, Cornell whipped around to face Kane. Angry words shattered the night's calm. "Don't make a noise there, come along," the corporal ordered.[2] But before he could turn around, Cornell brought his musket to aim. The corporal turned just in time to witness Cornell fire nearly point-blank into Kane's gut, knocking him flat on his back. Stunned, the corporal asked Cornell if he'd fired that shot. "Yes, by God; I hope I have," was Cornell's flat reply.

Cornell's fellow soldiers immediately confined him in the fort's stockade. Kane died within two minutes. On learning that his shot had not only struck Kane but killed him, Cornell stated chillingly: "I don't care a damn, I hope I have."[3]

The next day, the jury of inquest charged Cornell with "wilful [*sic*] murder,"[4] and the private was remanded to the civil authority to await trial.

William Cornell was seventeen years old.

His lawyers, Rivers and Correns, disputed the entire court proceedings on the grounds that Cornell was wrongfully on trial before the circuit court of Rhode Island, as Fort Adams was federal property. The court, however, struck this down, claiming that "although the United States may well purchase and hold lands for public purposes, within the territorial limits of a state, this does not of itself oust the jurisdiction of sovereignty of such a state over the lands so purchased."[5] In other words, because the fort physically existed within the geographical territory of the state of Rhode Island, the state could claim jurisdiction over criminal activity on fort property. This determination may in fact have provided the basis for future cases involving Fort Adams, in which joint investigations between the military and the local police were conducted.[6]

When considering Cornell's mental ability to commit such an act, and whether premeditation was involved, it was revealed that "the soldiers in the garrison had received an extra gill of rum that day [of Kane's murder], being the customary allowance on the celebration of independence. But there was no evidence that they [Cornell and Kane] were intoxicated."[7] This would not be the last time that alcohol would be suggested as the culprit in a tragedy at Fort Adams. The specter of liquor addiction would raise its head again and again through the years whenever a killing or a suicide occurred. But in this case, if liquor was not to blame, the guilt lay squarely on Cornell's own personality. He "was proved to be illiterate, and badly educated, and of an irascible temper." As to Cornell's being provoked by Kane's laughter and throwing of small bits of gravel at his back, the court remarked, "It did not appear that there was any injury to the prisoner [Cornell] by the throwing of it [the gravel]"; and the court also stated that Kane's taunts were not sufficient to justify Cornell's extreme reaction and reduce the charge to manslaughter resulting from a passion of temper. In the court's view, Cornell had acted out of all proportion to Kane's offense, used a weapon specifically intended for the ending of human life and expressed intent to kill not only in his previous quarrel with Kane but also in his comments after the shooting. Nor was Cornell's naturally hot temper considered an excuse for his action. A person capable of being provoked so easily and quickly as Cornell showed himself to be was a danger and a menace. In November, the court determined that Cornell had been motivated by "a brutal and diabolical malignity…a cruel and revengeful disposition." The jury pronounced him guilty of murder in the first degree, and the judge sentenced him to death by hanging.

In September 1820, however, Cornell surprisingly received a two-month stay of execution.[8] Finally, in late November of that year, practically on the eve of Cornell's execution, when preparations for his death were being made, President James Monroe issued a presidential pardon and Cornell was free from any further repercussions of his crime.[9] On June 28, 1820, the *Providence Patriot* reported that Cornell's mother was planning a journey to Washington to petition the president for her son's life. Did she make that trip? Did she succeed in gaining the ear of President Monroe, and was he swayed by the pathos of a mother's tears for her child?

William Cornell lived on and faded from history. His name never appeared again in connection with any violence. Yet he was not the first of his line to be associated with an atrocity, nor would he be the last. William's ancestors had been under the shadow of violent murder long before, since the death of elderly Rebecca Cornell on February 8, 1673.[10]

The Cornells were members of one of the most prominent families in Rhode Island, having been among the earliest settlers of the town of Portsmouth, Newport's neighbor to the north, in 1638. In 1673, Rebecca Cornell was living quietly on her Portsmouth farm with her son Thomas and his wife and children, until her sudden death before her own hearth. When her family went to her room to summon her to dinner, they discovered the poor woman's charred remains lying on the floor, close to the fireplace. At the time, the coroner determined that Rebecca had been dozing in her chair before the fire when a spark caught her skirts and set them aflame.

After Rebecca was buried, her brother approached authorities with an unbelievable tale. He claimed that his dead sister had appeared to him in a dream, stood at the side of his bed, and said, "See how I was Burnt with fire."[11] Rebecca's body was exhumed (a very severe recourse in that time, as religious belief forbade disturbing the dead for any reason) and reexamined. Astonishingly, a hole was found in her chest, near the heart. The cause of death was changed: Rebecca had been burned, surely—but only after a killer had thrust a fire poker through her heart.

Rebecca's own son Thomas was arrested and tried for his mother's murder, the prosecution defining his motive as the gaining of her property. Though Thomas Cornell never wavered in proclaiming his innocence, he was convicted and hanged in Newport on May 23, 1673.[12]

Thomas Cornell's wife, Sarah, was pregnant at the time of her husband's execution. The baby girl she later bore was christened Innocent Cornell, who grew up to marry the scion of another founding family of New England, Richard Borden. Through their line, in 1860, another baby girl was born: Lizzie Andrew Borden, the woman forever immortalized in jump-rope rhyme as the inhuman hatchet-murderess of her own father and stepmother. Though Lizzie was acquitted and lived out the remainder of her life without reproach, the pall of suspected guilt never lifted from this infamous Cornell descendant.[13]

But perhaps this beleaguered family has gotten the proverbial bad rap. Others, including Thomas's wife, Sarah, were suspected of Rebecca Cornell's murder, raising the possibility that Thomas, who denied his guilt to his final breath, may indeed have been innocent.[14] And his direct descendant Lizzie Borden was never proved to be a murderess, either. It may well be that the reputation of the Cornells as a family of killers is undeserved and that the only Cornell to have truly committed murder was Fort Adams' own William, in 1819.

A Tragic Legacy

Cornell's murder of Kane was the first reported intentional spilling of blood on the soil of Fort Adams. Unfortunately, this first murder would provide a pattern for two future killings, one attempted murder and no fewer than six suicides.

The "old" Fort Adams that Kane and Cornell called home was replaced in 1824 by the massive fortification that can be visited today. It was this structure that witnessed the next violent ending of life, on July 24, 1871, when twenty-eight-year-old George F. Drake of Company L, Fifth Artillery, whose real name was H.E. Lourie, slit his own throat "from ear to ear" in a state of despair after his sweetheart ended their relationship.[15] "The disappointment," remarked the *Newport Mercury*, had "rendered him partially insane."

The grave of H.E. Lourie in the Fort Adams cemetery, showing the assumed name under which he enlisted: George F. Drake.

Three years later, in early August of 1874, a man named Kerrigan was arrested for desertion after going AWOL from Fort Adams and spending time at the home of his parents in Providence.[16] Like the unfortunate Lourie, Kerrigan had enlisted under an assumed name, Henry Howard, and it was this name by which he was known among his comrades. Late in the afternoon of Thursday, August 7, 1874, Howard was one of three army prisoners shackled by ball and chain, enduring the sweaty work of chopping wood by axe under the hot summer sun, with no trees to shade them, as part of their disciplinary work detail. Only one guard, "a small man and a new recruit by the name of Cassidy," stood watch over the three prisoners.

The problem with giving an axe to a man wearing a ball and chain is that his minders have placed a tool for his liberation into his hands, and he is hardly likely to restrict his activities to chopping wood if desertion is on his mind to begin with.

At around 4:00 p.m., Howard broke his bonds, probably by employing the axe in some way. The instant the axe fell from his hands, he rushed the sole guard that had been placed in charge of him and his fellow prisoners, shouting, "We might as well have it out now!"

The inexperienced Cassidy was unprepared, unequipped and no physical match for the "large and powerful" Howard. Shocked, he couldn't react before Howard's arm was around his throat and wrestling him to the ground. Cassidy felt his rifle being pulled from him, and he tightened his grip, thinking that if Howard wrested it from him he would never see another day. Fighting for his very life, he cried out for help at the top of his voice. Now the stakes were raised: instead of dealing with only one runty, green recruit, Howard would soon be facing the sergeant of the guard, who would bring others as well. Desperate to shut Cassidy up, Howard slammed his fist into the man's face again and again. But even with this pummeling, the guard's iron grasp on his rifle would not let up. Howard gave up on the gun and turned to the bayonet on the end of its barrel, pulling at the fitting. Although Cassidy must have felt that Howard was trying to seize his weapon in order to kill him, as the *Newport Daily News* account suggested,[17] the fact that Howard dropped his axe before attacking the guard may have indicated that he only wanted to disarm the man in order to guarantee a safe escape. Had Howard intended to kill, he would surely have held on to the axe and brandished it at Cassidy.

Suddenly, perhaps fearing that help would arrive at any moment in response to Cassidy's continuous shouts, Howard stopped struggling, released the guard's weapon and tore across the ditch toward the sally port at a dead run. The stunned, battered guard scrabbled to his feet, collected himself enough to stand, took aim and loosed a bullet directly into the left hip of the fast-moving prisoner.

Assistance finally arrived in the person of one Captain Willard, who had heard the guard's shot ring out and came running to investigate its cause. When Willard opened Howard's shirt and found that the rifle ball had ripped right through him, exiting through his right side, he knew the man's time was very short and told him as much. Willard asked if Howard wanted to convey any final words to anyone, but he couldn't make out Howard's reply. When the guard told Willard what had happened and the captain asked Howard if he had indeed attacked the guard, to his credit, Howard offered the truth. It would be his final communication: he was dead before he could be transferred to the infirmary.

Cassidy was never the same after killing Howard. Only three months later, an officer returning from leave noticed that Cassidy was absent from his post—and worse, had left his weapon behind. The officer found him leaving the sutler's store in possession of some items he had not troubled

Howard's grave, Fort Adams cemetery.

to purchase. Cassidy, who had been commended by his superiors for his actions in dealing with Howard, was now court-martialed and sentenced to a prison term in Albany Penitentiary. The man who had killed a prisoner for attempting to escape was now a prisoner himself.

While the killing of Howard can't be called murder, as Private Cassidy had acted in the regrettable circumstance of preserving his own life as well as doing his duty, the next man to lose his life at Fort Adams certainly was the victim of deliberate foul play.

On Saturday, November 15, 1879, Private Franz Koppe[18] of Light Battery K, a Berlin-born Prussian stonecutter and twenty-year veteran of the United States Army, went into the town of Newport with some comrades to enjoy an afternoon's leave, their soldier's pay fresh in their hands.[19] They returned to Fort Adams that same evening. Koppe was well liked by his comrades in every post to which he'd been assigned, known as a "modest and unassuming… quiet and inoffensive man," a "peaceable man."[20] Before being stationed at Fort Adams, he had served with honor in the brutal Civil War battles of Cold Harbor[21] and the Wilderness. But despite his sterling record and mild personality, like many of his fellow soldiers, Koppe was known to frequently drink too much, and he had been drinking quite a lot that Saturday in 1879, not only during his leave but even after his return to the fort. At a little before 9:00 p.m., Koppe visited the post sutler, where he ran into Corporal William Nicholson. The two men had served together in Battery F previously, and

The southwest postern, a candidate for the location of the murder of Private Franz Koppe.

in an eerie similarity to the relationship between Kane and Cornell, had, to all appearances, been friends throughout that time. But witnesses later testified that on this night, in the sutler's store, Nicholson asked Koppe when the private was going to pay back some money he'd borrowed. Though the witnesses reported this exchange as a civil one, another far more sinister encounter would occur later that night that would throw Nicholson under suspicion of murder.

After 9:00 p.m., as Sergeant John Brown passed the sally port between the barracks of Companies E and F, he heard raised voices. On approaching their source, he discovered Koppe and Nicholson in the heat of an argument, Nicholson appearing especially irate. Both men reeked of alcohol, with Koppe seeming a great deal more under the influence than Nicholson. The sergeant tried to break up the scene by ordering both men to their barracks and to bed, reminding Koppe that his duty required him to rise only a few hours later, at 3:00 a.m. A relieved Koppe gladly agreed, but Nicholson threatened that Koppe wasn't going anywhere until he paid his debt. When Koppe denied owing Nicholson any such debt, the corporal insisted angrily,

"Yes, you do, you owe me three dollars."[22] Koppe, eager to escape, simply replied that the matter could wait—he wasn't going to talk about it tonight.

Once again, Sergeant Brown ordered Koppe to turn in for the night. But just as the private finally turned to go, Nicholson stopped him by grabbing his left arm. At this point, Brown left them, perhaps realizing that he wasn't going to get anywhere with his entreaties and leaving the two friends to settle their own differences in the form of a drunken brawl. As he walked away, he noted that Koppe did leave Nicholson, probably to go to his barracks. But later that night, Brown would hear a noise "like the falling of barrels in the bakery,"[23] and he would have reason to recall this sound in a court of law.

Meanwhile, one Sergeant Lane was on duty when he heard noises and "scuffling"[24] in the sally port. Moving toward the sounds, he heard Nicholson's voice cry over and over, "God damn you, Koppe!" Shortly after these words rang out, Sergeant Lane heard more scuffling in the same area, followed by the sound of the stone lid closing over the cistern just outside the gate. Lane thought nothing of this, as the closing of this cover was a normal and familiar sound: true, the cistern was usually left open so its water could be accessed, but of course it was also closed occasionally. Besides, noises frequently echoed in and around that sally port, where sound had a tendency to reverberate strangely. Eventually, the scuffling sounds stopped, and Nicholson's voice was no longer heard. Silence reigned once more. Suspecting nothing untoward, as all of these noises could be accounted for in the course of normal activity, Sergeant Lane carried on his business.

About six hours later, at 3:00 a.m., a soldier of Company F was passing near the sally port by his company's barracks when he heard a curious sound. Stopping to investigate, he determined that the sounds were the cries of a human voice—and they were coming from the cistern beyond the wall.

Running to the spot, the soldier noticed that the large, heavy stone lid was covering the cistern's opening. That same cistern had certainly been seen open six hours before. As the soldier drew nearer, the cries became louder, calling for help from within the sealed pit. How anyone could have survived down there was nothing short of a miracle, as placing the stone cover would have cut off any source of air. But when the soldier struggled to remove the stone, sure enough he discovered a man clinging to the stone steps that led down into the water.

It was Franz Koppe.

The soldier who found Koppe called for help, and others responded immediately to rescue their comrade. When Koppe finally emerged, the full horror of his condition was revealed: dried blood completely obscured

The imposing north wall is another possible site for Koppe's murder. The north gate fits Sergeant Lane's description of an echoey sally port.

This morbidly humorous image warns soldiers of the dangers of inebriation. *Fort Adams Trust.*

his head and features, as if someone had deliberately inflicted wounds meant to be fatal before throwing him into the cistern and shutting its lid. Or worse—perhaps Koppe's assailant had only intended to knock him unconscious, planning for him to come around inside the cistern and be aware of what was happening as he died a slow, suffocating death.

Several hours later, when Sergeant Brown, who had tried to prevent violence between Koppe and Nicholson the night before, heard that the private had been "cut" about the face and head, he sought Koppe out and found him in the mess hall kitchen. Amazingly, Koppe was able to walk on his own. On seeing the man's terrible state, Sergeant Brown ordered him to the infirmary. But before Koppe could comply, who should arrive in the kitchen but Corporal Nicholson. Brown saw him say something to Koppe, but the battered private didn't acknowledge Nicholson's words. Koppe then proceeded to the infirmary, where he arrived at about 7:30 a.m. There, Koppe, accompanied by an orderly but walking and standing on his own power, told Dr. J.F. Hammond that he was "sick." Dr. Hammond escorted Koppe to a bed and asked him what had happened. Koppe only answered that on his way to his barracks from the sutler the previous evening, he'd tripped over a rock and hit his head on another rock, due to his drinking a great quantity of beer.

But something was clearly wrong with Koppe's simple account. A single strike of the head on a single rock would not have caused the massive injuries Dr. Hammond observed on Koppe's head and face:

> *He had a severe contused wound over the right eye. The lids were blackened and swollen; about an inch above the right eyebrow there was an abrasion of the skin extending horizontally; one inch above that was a lacerated contused wound, extending about two inches horizontally; this wound extended to the scalp and through the periosteum; there was also an abrasion of the skin anterior on the top of the skull; this was circular, about one half inch in diameter; there was another abrasion about the middle of the right side of the head; there was also an abrasion between the eye and the ear on the right side; there was also an abrasion on the right cheek near the lower jaw bone…These contusions and abrasions were all on the right side except one and that on a medium line just above the forehead. The abrsuions* [sic] *were all apparently made by a rough surface such as would be made by a rough stone similar to a grind-stone. The contused wound on the head and periosity apparently made by a blunt stone.*[25]

Still, the doctor believed at the time that Koppe was no more than another solider "recovering from a drunken spree."[26] He treated Koppe's lacerations and prescribed medication and rest in the infirmary, promising to check in on the private as often as he was able.

Later that morning, Sergeant Lane made his way to the mess hall kitchen, where the cook, who had already seen Koppe, filled him in on what had happened to the unfortunate private. Lane recalled Nicholson's words of the previous night and the sounds he'd heard near the sally port and told the cook about his experience, wondering if there might be a connection. Lane was then informed that he "would get into trouble for what he said about the affair."[27]

In the infirmary, Koppe appeared at first to be making a recovery. The "salts" prescribed by Dr. Hammond seemed to do the trick, and the next day (Monday, November 17), Koppe himself coherently told the doctor that he felt better. He even "had strength enough to walk to the water-closet without assistance."[28] But toward afternoon, the nurse informed Dr. Hammond that on his last visit to Koppe's room, he noticed that Koppe had taken off all his bandages and replaced them in different areas. At around 2:00 p.m., a similar episode repeated itself when Koppe was seen "pulling" at his bandages. These were bad signs—indications "that his mind seemed to be affected."[29] When Dr. Hammond took Koppe's temperature, it registered between 102° and 105°. By 5:20 p.m., Koppe's body temp was 105.6°. Whether the raging fever was due to an onset of infection in his wounds or to swelling of his brain as a result of his extensive injuries, or some combination of both, nothing further could be done for him. Koppe's life ended at 9:20 p.m. on Monday night, November 17, after suffering unimaginably for two days and three nights.[30]

After a court of inquiry held at the fort, William Nicholson was arrested for the murder of his former friend and confined in the fort's stockade.[31] Because Koppe was not dead when he was found in the cistern, United States Commissioner Colonel William Gilpin's desire that an inquest take place was not granted. However, the day after Koppe's death, Colonel Gilpin issued a formal complaint against Corporal Nicholson to U.S. District Attorney Nathan F. Dixon in a joint investigation between military and civil judicial authorities. At the preliminary hearing, Sergeants Lane and Brown offered dramatic testimony of the altercations between Koppe and Nicholson, and Dr. Hammond provided the gruesome technical facts of Koppe's physical condition. When the proceedings concluded, District Attorney Nixon determined to send Nicholson's case to the grand jury to

The tilted, lichen-covered gravestone of murder victim Franz Koppe in the Fort Adams cemetery.

Fort Adams' stockade, circa late 1860s to early 1870s. *National Archives; acquired courtesy of Daniel P. Titus.*

Fort Adams' jail today, fully restored and housing the gift shop and Fort Adams Trust offices.

establish or rule out grounds for a full criminal trial. Nicholson took leave of his young wife at the courthouse and then returned to the stockade at Fort Adams to await the convening of the grand jury.

A little more than a week later, on the morning of December 12, 1879, Deputy U.S. Marshal Knowles ordered the corporal released from imprisonment, and Nicholson resumed his regular duties at the Fort Adams garrison.[32] The grand jury had declined to send the case to trial.

How did Koppe really die? His death record states the cause as simply "Contused & Lacerated Wound,"[33] betraying no hint of foul play. One contemporary account energetically reported that no one observing the preliminary hearing could believe Nicholson capable of such an atrocity: he possessed the bearing of "a very manly and intelligent appearing soldier, and made a favorable impression upon all who saw him."[34] Was he falsely accused? Did Nicholson, after many times cursing his friend with the loud and angry words, "God damn you, Koppe!" simply storm off to his barracks to sleep off his drunkenness and his rage? Did Koppe, in his own inebriated state, fall into the cistern while trying to get back to his own barracks? Did he perhaps make it to his bed but remained so hungover and sleep-deprived that he accidentally fell into the cistern when he rose and tried to report for duty at 3:00 a.m., the time he was found half-dead? Did an innocent passerby unwittingly close the cistern lid, unaware that the then-unconscious Koppe was inside? Did Nicholson impulsively push Koppe into the cistern and then, in terror and guilt, close the lid in order to hide his deadly error? Or did the corporal deliberately bash Koppe's head in and maliciously cast him into the pit?

We will never know. There is no record of anyone else ever being formally accused of Koppe's murder. Beneath the weathered, lichen-spotted gravestone of Franz Koppe in the Fort Adams cemetery lies a mystery that will likely remain buried forever.

"O that the Everlasting had not fix'd/His cannon 'gainst self-slaughter!"

—*Hamlet*, I.ii.1 4

After Koppe's murder, the Fort Adams community down through the succeeding years experienced a rash of suicides. On Tuesday, December 28, 1886, First Lieutenant James M. Jones, a man "exceedingly popular with his fellows," was despondent over the prospect of facing military discipline after being on leave eight days too long.[35] After Jones consumed a hearty breakfast at about 8:00 a.m.—one hour before his scheduled appointment with the fort's commanding officer—a workman entered his quarters to do some scheduled repairs. Jones dismissed him, saying that he wanted to talk to the quartermaster before any work was done. The workman accordingly left and must have repeated this to the quartermaster, because the latter took it upon himself to initiate conversation by going to see Jones. But when the quartermaster entered the first lieutenant's rooms, he discovered the man lying senseless on the floor. He had shot himself in the back of the head.

Incredibly, Jones survived with this head wound throughout Tuesday and for the next four days. His agony must have been unimaginable before he finally expired on the night of Saturday, January 2. Unfortunately, his request that his remains be cremated was not honored, as it was "believed that he was not in his right mind" when he made it during the course of his suffering.[36]

At the end of that same year, on December 21, forty-year-old First Sergeant Robert Walker of Battery B was in the same situation as Jones: waiting in his quarters for a dreaded appointment.[37] He was to be disciplined for an infraction that he feared might cost him his stripes and demote him back to the ranks. At 9:00 a.m., he would face his captain to learn his fate. But he refused to keep the meeting. After Walker failed to report, the sergeant of the guard set out to bring him forcibly before the captain. The instant he reached Walker's door, the first sergeant shot himself dead with a .45-caliber revolver to his right temple.

Private Peter Gorman followed on Sunday, August 28, 1898, slitting his own throat with his razor after coming home from a leave spent in Brooklyn.[38] The only motive considered for the suicide was that Gorman had been drinking a great deal during his leave and that "his nerves were unstrung." He lingered until the following day, but before dying on the afternoon of Monday, August 29, "when he learned he was to die he showed by his action that the act was unpremeditated." It is difficult to imagine how a person might not premeditate the action or consequences of cutting his own throat, but if this was true in Gorman's case, his death is all the more tragic.

On August 23, 1901, Private John A. Yeager, who'd been noticeably depressed for several days, told his comrades that he felt too ill to go on drill with them.[39] When the last man of his company was gone, Yeager shot himself to death with his rifle.

Six years later, on the night of Saturday, March 9, 1907, Private Timothy Richard Langdon was sitting at a table with his friends in their second-story brick barracks, which had been added to the top of Fort Adams' southeast wall the previous year to serve as living quarters for lower-ranking enlisted men.[40] Suddenly, and for no apparent reason, Langdon sprang up from his chair, rushed to a window and threw himself out of it, striking the rail of the exterior iron staircase before hitting the ground of the dry moat more than forty feet below. His companions immediately ran to his aid and found, incredibly, that Langdon was still alive. They rushed him to the infirmary, but Langdon's fractured skull, severe concussion and internal injuries were beyond help. He clung to life for a full day, never regaining consciousness, before dying some time after noon on Monday, March 11. Once again, excessive drinking was blamed. At the time, Fort Adams officers "advance[d] the theory that had there been a canteen

Left: The gravestone of suicide victim First Sergeant Robert Walker, Fort Adams cemetery.

Below: Peter Gorman's grave, Fort Adams cemetery.

The grave of Private John A. Yeager in the cemetery at Fort Adams.

Formal company photograph, early 1900s, with iron balcony for the new enlisted men's barracks. *Sergeant Thomas A. Foshey Collection; courtesy of the Fort Adams Trust.*

Balcony and barracks, 1920s. *Fort Adams Trust.*

All that remains of the iron balcony today.

Interior ditch. The remaining wall of the upper-story barracks appears in the right distance. Here, both Private Langdon and Private Lajoie (see Chapter 3) fell to their deaths.

on the post this would not have happened, or he would have only been drinking pure liquors and would not have been allowed to drink enough to become intoxicated."[41]

Domestic Unrest

Fort Adams was not only home to soldiers. Officers' and enlisted men's children, mothers, sisters and wives also made their home within the fort's walls. Long ago, those granite walls resounded with the laughter of children at play, the chatter of officers' wives and the bustle of daily housework. Fort Adams was not only a military base: it was truly a community, a small town in and of itself. Babies came into the world and grew up, friends crossed the parade field to visit one another's homes and children ran through the length of their playmates' quarters along the east wall. In the garrison's chapel, marriages were solemnized and

This informal company photo from the early 1900s shows soldiers relaxing with their buddies. *Sergeant Thomas A. Foshey Collection; courtesy of the Fort Adams Trust.*

families attended Sunday services. Fort Adams' baseball and football teams competed with military and neighborhood civilian leagues alike, and community dances and regimental band concerts invited Newport's residents to enjoy social gatherings in the fort's unique and beautiful setting. The deaths that occurred throughout the years were only a part of the larger life that thrived in this place. The garrison's cemetery bears witness that not only soldiers lived and died here: of those graves, 11 percent contain the remains of women, and a surprising and poignant 28 percent belong to babies and children.[42]

Living conditions, especially in the fort's early years, were positively dreadful. Brick and stone cannon casemates were converted into housing, with few improvements at first. Very little light ever managed to get through the "windows," which were little more than narrow rifle loopholes. These converted casemates were havens for damp, cold and condensation, highly subject to mildew. In such conditions, there's little wonder that disease was such a frequent occurrence at Fort Adams. Later, around the time of the Civil War, conditions improved when casemates were lined with lath and plaster walls, fireplaces and Dutch ovens were installed, and raised wooden floors were put in. These amenities were quite elegant, featuring ornate moldings and pocket doors that could easily compare with the decorative workmanship in any high-society Newport home of the time. In the late 1870s, new houses were built for the officers and their families beyond the land defenses to the south. "Officer's Row" still stands today and serves as housing for the families of navy officers.[43] From 1900 to 1950, the year Fort Adams was decommissioned, the former officers' quarters within the fort proper were used as living space once again, this time for the fort's senior-ranking enlisted men.

It was during this period that a Fort Adams corporal did the unthinkable. On Thursday, December 31, 1908, Ellen Henry, the twenty-six-year-old wife of Fort Adams band member Corporal Nelson Henry, was recovering from the birth of her third child the day before.[44] The corporal had gone into town to buy clothing and shoes for the couple's two older daughters, ages five and three. When he returned at a little after 3:00 p.m., the baby's nurse took the infant into another part of the family's quarters, perhaps to allow Ellen some time to rest or to allow a private conversation between husband and wife. Corporal Henry entered the bedroom, closing the door behind him. He confronted Ellen with suspicions that she'd been unfaithful to him, saying that the baby born just the day before wasn't his. As Ellen lay in her bed, her husband shot her three times in the chest, arm and shoulder. Remaining in the room, Henry then placed the gun's barrel against his own temple and fired.

Those who ran to investigate the source of the shots discovered Mrs. Henry "lying on the floor unconscious with blood pouring from her wounds."[45] The corporal was already dead.

The *Newport Mercury* for Saturday, January 2, 1909, stated that this awful occurrence was "a great shock to the officers and men at the post," but according to the same article, Mrs. Henry had previously voiced fears about her husband, even to the point that he "might sometime injure her, as his temper was apt to get the better of him."[46]

As their mother struggled for her life, all three of the Henry family's little ones entered the care of family friends who also lived at the fort. Ellen was not expected to live. Although the fort's physicians were making every effort their skill and the era's medical technology allowed, they held little hope and believed her wounds would in the end prove fatal. There was every indication that her little children would soon be completely orphaned.

Yet miraculously, on January 2, the day of the corporal's funeral, the *Newport Daily News* reported that Ellen Henry was recovering against all

The gravestone of suicide and almost-murderer Corporal Nelson Henry in the Fort Adams cemetery.

odds. At the same time, Corporal Henry's bandmates were planning to hold a benefit concert, inviting the larger Newport community, to raise funds in support of the widow and for the care of her children. Four days after the shooting, Ellen was expected to make a full recovery, displaying the remarkable strength of a mother who will trample down death itself for the sake of her children. The *Newport Daily News* of January 4 stated that "the women of the garrison are showing her every possible attention," donations were being solicited for the family and commanding officer Captain Walter Howe had "appointed a board to learn if the deceased lost his life while in the service of his country, for in that case his family would be given a pension."[47] According to army records, that pension was indeed granted on March 25, 1909.[48]

As tragic as this episode was, it had a happy ending after all. The stories in this chapter have shown that Fort Adams was a place of despair, jealousy and homicidal fury, but the story of the Henry family also proves that Fort Adams was a place where people banded together in the face of hardship. It was a community of caring men and women who, without being asked, stepped up to help their neighbors in times of desperate need. Like any civilian community, it was home to sinners and villains but also to saints and heroes. And if the memories of darkness and tragedy linger on there, surely the bright light of these human kindnesses still shines bravely within them.

Chapter 2

"Hurried into Eternity"[49]

Death from the Deep

A Terrible Beauty

The waters surrounding Newport are among the most beautiful in the world and among the most favorable for sailing. The "City by the Sea" has long been a destination for recreational and sport boating alike. President John F. Kennedy himself plied the waters of Narragansett Bay while summering at Hammersmith Farm, the ancestral home of First Lady Jackie's stepfather Hugh Auchincloss, whose land abutted the property of Fort Adams. The oldest race in sailing, the America's Cup, was held in Newport waters for more than 130 years, until the Australian team seized the trophy in 1983 after a long rivalry with the Newport-based New York Yacht Club, which had held the prize since the cup's inception in 1851.[50] Aquidneck Island's beaches are jam-packed every season with families, swimmers and surfers—Newport's beach culture borders on pseudo-tropical. But unless visitors (or locals, for that matter) travel out to Fort Adams for a tour and learn something of the harbor's violent history, they would likely remain unaware of the fact that the pleasant waters in which they swim, surf and sail required the protection of the greatest artillery fortification on the East Coast.

Newport Harbor is the reason for Fort Adams' existence.[51] As the largest natural deep-water harbor between Boston and New York, the port provided a bustling haven for merchant ships, making Newport one of the major cities in the American colonies prior to the Revolution, on a close par in wealth with New York, Boston and Philadelphia. When the war began, all that

Newport Harbor today, from Fort Adams. Lime Rock Lighthouse (now the private Ida Lewis Yacht Club) is the small white house on the far right.

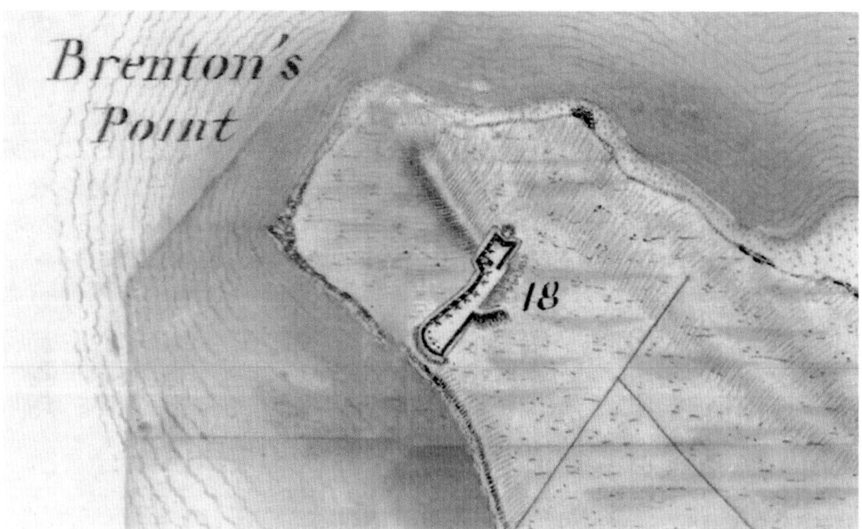

Revolution-era French map showing the earthworks on the future site of Fort Adams. *National Archives; acquired courtesy of Daniel P. Titus.*

changed. Newport Harbor, so attractive to traders (and pirates), was coveted by the British Royal Navy for the very same reasons: the size and depth of the harbor offered an ideal home base for a great fleet of warships, and the city's location would allow access by sea to the entire East Coast. In April 1776, British vessels of war entered Newport Harbor seeking to possess this highly strategic place. The Newport Artillery Company, the oldest militia in the United States still active today, established an earthworks artillery battery at Brenton's Point—the future site of Fort Adams—to repel the invading ships. On two separate occasions—April 6 and 10, 1776—the invading ships approached the harbor, and both times the guns on the Point drove them into retreat. This furlough gave Newport the leeway to declare on May 4 that the colony of Rhode Island and Providence Plantations would no longer pay allegiance to the King of England—the first colony to make such a move.

But this independence was short-lived. The British would not relent in their efforts to secure this strategic port city. In the end, Newport was unable to hold its freedom. On December 8, 1776, the British sailed up the poorly defended west passage of Narragansett Bay, on the far side of Jamestown, Newport's neighbor on Conanicut Island to the west, and hooked around Jamestown's northern end to enter Newport Harbor. The British Twenty-second Regiment landed and seized the city, quartering its troops in private homes, some of which stand to this day. The regiment also seized the batteries at Brenton's Point and Goat Island across the harbor. For the next three years, Newport experienced one of the harshest occupations of the war.

At last, in July 1778, the French fleet under the Comte d'Estaing mounted a relief effort. After blockading Aquidneck Island to the south, the French expressed plans for an outright invasion of Newport Harbor, scaring the British into scuttling their own vessels to make the harbor impassable—a massive loss of transportation and firepower. The British were now stranded in the city and surrounded by hostile forces. Technically, Newport was still occupied.

Ultimately, though, the French initiative was a failure. Their effort was hampered by status-seeking among French commanders D'Estaing and the Marquis de Lafayette and essentially ended altogether by great damage to their vessels. August 9 saw the arrival of British naval reinforcements under Admiral Howe and an ensuing firefight; a brutal two-day storm immediately following this action effectively crippled the French force. In order to repair their ships—and to avoid further engagement with Howe—the French departed Rhode Island waters and sailed to Boston on August 20, abandoning

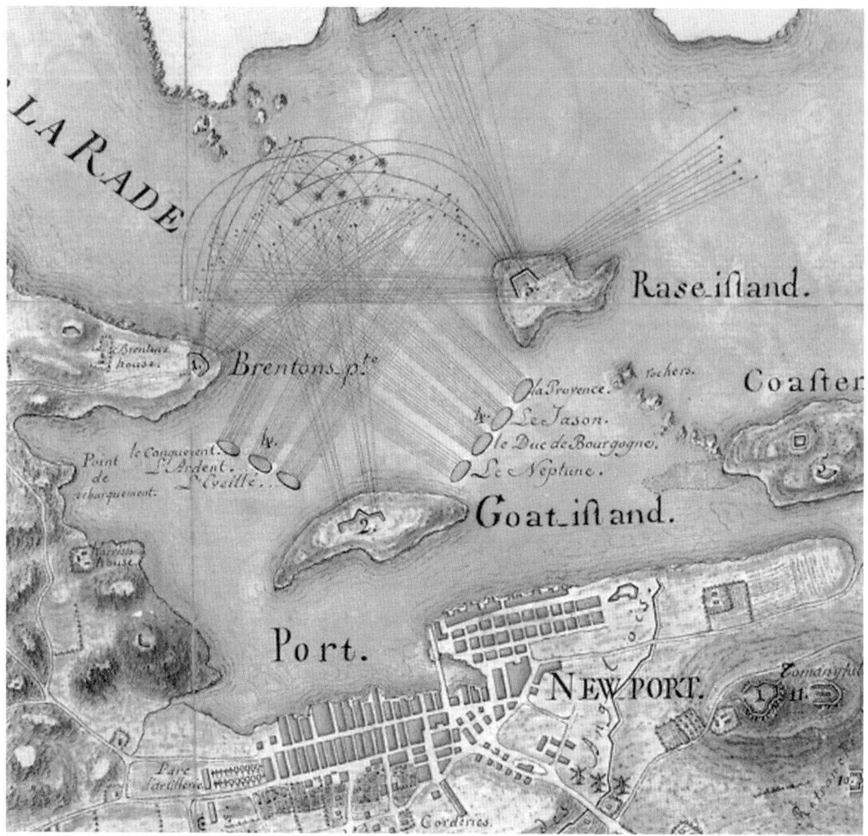

Newport Harbor defenses, in a French map, circa 1780. *National Archives; acquired courtesy of Daniel P. Titus.*

Newport once again to the mercy of the increasingly strengthening British presence. Soon after d'Estaing's departure, Continental forces besieged Newport by land but were routed northwards right across Aquidneck Island and over the Sakonnet River in the August 29 Battle of Rhode Island.[52]

The grip of the Crown's regiments did not let up until 1779, when the red-coat troops were called away from Newport to reinforce positions in the southern colonies, but their departure failed to lift the pall of despair and failure their occupation had laid over the city. Newport's economy never fully recovered. Its status as a major East Coast port was gone. Never wanting the city to experience such a devastating blow again, the government constructed the original Fort Adams in 1799. This was the small fort that saw the Cornell-Kane incident. It would stand until the new fort's construction began in 1824.

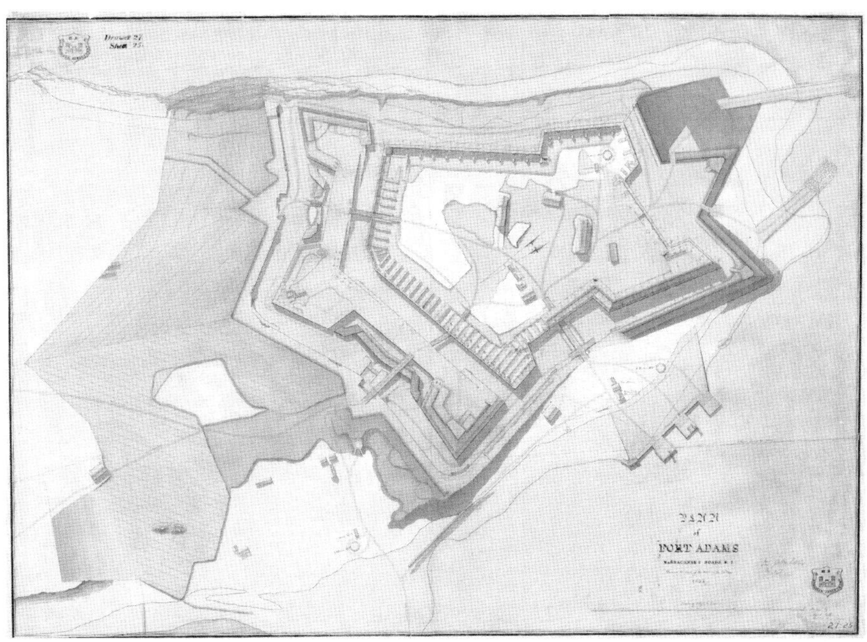

Plan of work for the second Fort Adams, 1833. *National Archives; compiled by Bolling W. Smith and acquired courtesy of John T. Duchesneau.*

When war loomed again in 1812, the British Royal Navy once more threatened the East Coast. But this time, even though Fort Adams was manned by three militia companies, the Crown's ships did not land at Newport. They stayed off shore, forming a strangling blockade,[53] but they did land farther south at Washington, and royal troops razed the young capital to the ground. After the United States declared victory in that conflict, the federal government was spurred to action. Congress established a Fortifications Board in 1816 to develop a series of defenses along the entire eastern seaboard. This was the beginning of the Coast Artillery Corps of the United States Army. Still remembering the part Newport Harbor had played in the Revolution, the Fortifications Board selected Newport as one of the locations whose defenses would receive a facelift. The old Fort Adams was declared inadequate to properly defend the area in case of attack, and by this time it was falling into disrepair. Rather than shore it up, the board decided to tear it down and start from scratch to construct the largest and most complex fortification in North America at that time: a defensive work so intimidating that none would dare attack it. By safeguarding Newport Harbor and preventing any future enemy from establishing a base (as the

British had done in 1776), the new Fort Adams would indirectly defend the entire East Coast.

The view of Newport Harbor from the top of the fort's northeast bastion is nothing less than breathtaking, but as tour guests gaze on the golden crystalline brilliance of blue water under vast blue sky, the quaint docks across the way, sailboats of all sizes skimming past and the green islands surrounding them, most aren't aware of just how treacherous those beautiful waters are, their history of warfare and the many untimely and freakish deaths that those waters have witnessed.

Perished at Sea

On June 17, 1826, the body of one Oliver Gragg Jr. was found floating in the waters near Fort Adams. Apparently, Gragg had taken his sailboat on a leisurely jaunt from Boston to Newport, and the vessel had capsized in the waters of the harbor.[54] Almost exactly one year later, a similar incident occurred, this time involving a Providence fishing boat that had arrived in the waters off the town of Portsmouth, at the northernmost end of Aquidneck Island, and was overcome by a storm on May 8, 1827.[55] This event had gruesome repercussions, as waterlogged corpses and the articles that had belonged to them in life continued to drift ashore on beaches in Portsmouth and Newport periodically for more than a month. On May 25, the Providence newspaper *Rhode-Island American* claimed that the body of one of the victims had come to rest near Portsmouth's coal mine wharf. The same article also published the names of the victims: Ladding Luther, Isaac U. Horton, Samuel Aldritch, James Bromley, Joseph Mason and Samuel Hopkins. On May 26, the *Newport Mercury* reported that "4 hats, 2 caps, a jug of liquor" and a "fish car" had all washed up at Portsmouth. Strangely, that paper also claimed that none of the remains had turned up, despite the report of the *Rhode-Island American* to the contrary. Then, on June 2, the *Mercury* reported that another body was found at Portsmouth, likely one of the victims of this tragedy at sea.

On June 9, the *Mercury* related that the drowned remains of Samuel Aldritch had drifted southward to Newport and come to rest in Coddington's Cove, close to the north end of the harbor. Yet another drowned corpse had been discovered at Portsmouth, unidentifiable except for the letters "A.L." embroidered on a silk handkerchief at the man's waist. These initials do not match the names of any of the victims of this boating tragedy, so two possibilities arise: either he was not among this group of men from the Providence fishing boat, or A.L. were the initials of a loved one who had given the handkerchief to him.

Finally, on June 23, the *Mercury* published a brief notice regarding a corpse that had washed ashore close to Fort Adams. A coroner's inquest was conducted; the body was assumed to be one of the victims of the fishing boat accident. Nothing more was said of him. Where previous notices had described the victims' clothing, hair color and other articles, now there was no description. We can only imagine the state of decay this body must have been in after drifting in the waters of Narragansett Bay for a month and a half. The article concluded with a mention that the body had been buried at the Fort Adams cemetery. A 2001 study by Daniel P. Titus and Gerald Foley at Salve Regina University in Newport shows that the cemetery that exists at Fort Adams today was established shortly after the army garrison moved into the "new" Fort Adams in 1841, but the 1799 fort surely had some other location in which to bury its dead, having been active for twenty-five years.[56] The account of the drowning victim being interred at the cemetery of Fort Adams in 1827 bears out the idea that a graveyard did exist prior to 1841. Titus and Foley surmise that some time after the old fort was replaced by the new, the original cemetery was moved to its present location, which would of course include the moving of any human remains. The study also suggests that this relocation of graves may explain the mysterious tombstones marked "Unknown" in the present cemetery.[57] Do the remains of this drowned man from long ago lie in one of those graves?

We may never know. But we can know for certain that some of Fort Adams' own also succumbed to the deceptively gorgeous waters of Newport Harbor and Narragansett Bay.

One of these was John Cook, who was eighteen years old in 1863, at the height of the Civil War.[58] On September 16, two and a half months after the Battle of Gettysburg, a barge belonging to Fort Adams somehow got stranded on Goat Island, directly across from Fort Adams on the side of the harbor closest to the city. The captain of a boat called *Rebecca*, Patrick O'Connell, noticed the barge and duly notified the fort's commanding officer. A small unit of five men was sent to retrieve the barge under the command of Sergeant Smith. John Cook was among them. The Fort Adams men worked together with O'Connell and succeeded in freeing the barge and sending it into the water. It would have been a mission well and quickly done. But while Cook was assisting O'Connell to hoist *Rebecca*'s sail and haul in the sheet, a sloop called the *Greenpoint* appeared seemingly out of

Five graves in a row displaying the name "Unknown" in the Fort Adams cemetery. A total of fifteen stones bear this designation.

nowhere and inexplicably collided with the sailboat's port side. *Rebecca* sank instantly—and its sail came down on O'Connell and Cook, forcing them into the water along with the sailboat's cloven hull.

By some miracle of strength and effort, O'Connell managed to fight his way out from under the sail and broke through to the surface. A young man serving on a sloop called the *Phebe Ann* took notice of the incident and came to O'Connell's aid, rowing over in a small boat and pulling in the exhausted man.

The *Greenpoint* sailed on.

Later that evening, the *Rebecca* was taken from the water. When it was pulled to the docks and searched, John Cook's lifeless body was discovered under the forward deck.

The coroner, a man by the name of Wood, outright accused the *Greenpoint*'s captain of directly causing Cook's death through "gross carelessness." "We trust," commented the *Newport Mercury*, "there is some way of yet making [the *Greenpoint* captain] suffer for his carelessness."

The next Fort Adams man to meet his death in the waters off Brenton's Point was Peter Rice, "a man of excellent character" and principal musician

John Cook's headstone in Fort Adams' cemetery proclaims that he "was drowned in the performance of his duty, in the harbor of Newport."

Fort Adams' dock, built to facilitate movement of massive granite blocks during construction. Several drowned corpses have turned up here in years past.

Left: The elaborate gravestone of Peter Rice in Fort Adams' cemetery.

Below: The Ida Lewis Yacht Club (private), formerly Lime Rock lighthouse (left), with Goat Island, once the site of the torpedo station (right).

in the First Artillery Band.[59] He had vanished without a trace on Sunday, January 12, 1879; the following Tuesday, his band cap was found on the fort's wharf, and further search revealed his drowned body in the frigid water nearby. A wife was now a widow, and six children were without a father. Rice had joined the First Artillery in 1854, and at the outbreak of the Civil War, he had been "one of the little band who made so gallant a resistance at Fort Sumter." Rice "always spoke of the pride he felt in having fired the first gun from the fortress at the rebels, and this was an honor his comrades freely admitted belonged to him." What an irony that this noble soldier, who took a stand in the madness of combat and lived to tell the tale, was killed not by a bullet or by cannon fire but by a freak accident, overpowered not by enemy Confederates but by the beautiful waters of Newport Harbor.

Rice was followed to this watery grave by at least three more Fort Adams soldiers, who all perished in different incidents. In 1892, Newport Harbor was guarded by three lighthouses: Rose Island Light, Newport Harbor Light on the north end of Goat Island, and Lime Rock Light, a nondescript white cottage situated on a little spit of land spearing into the harbor between Fort Adams and the downtown wharves. This was the post of Ida Lewis, one of the country's handful of female lighthouse keepers and to this day one of Newport's most beloved citizens, whose courage in taking her little skiff onto dangerous waters in terrifying weather conditions was recognized and honored throughout the nation. During the half century that she tended the light, Lewis was credited with rescuing eighteen people—and that was only the official count.[60] The actual count was possibly higher.

Throughout Fort Adams' history, the men of the garrison frequently enjoyed leave in town by boating back and forth across the harbor, and on some occasions met with calamity on the trip. Before Ida Lewis's time, in 1842, two artillerymen by the names of Brown and Bush drowned when their sailboat capsized in the harbor.[61] We can only guess how many Fort Adams soldiers were grateful when Lewis held her tenure at Lime Rock. On one occasion in April of 1869, she saved the lives of a Sergeant Adams and Private McLaughlin, whose boat had a mishap in the midst of the harbor. To express their gratitude, the men of the fort rewarded Lewis with $218 two months later. On February 4, 1881, the fearless keeper would again come to the aid of two soldiers. This time, the inebriated victims committed the unthinkable foolishness of attempting to walk across the "frozen" harbor on their return to the fort after a day in town. Ida Lewis spotted them from a kitchen window of the lighthouse and watched as both men crashed through the unstable ice. Without a moment's hesitation, Lewis hiked up her skirts and ran to the men's aid, herself venturing out onto ice she well knew to be treacherous. Incredibly, she literally reeled them both in with a length of clothesline, nearly losing her own life when the panicking soldiers pulled so hard on the line that Lewis too fell forward and through the ice, her heavy, layered nineteenth-century women's clothing dragging her down in the arctic water. But through sheer grit, steely nerve and force of will, she pulled herself out and finally succeeded in hauling both men to safety. As a direct result of this act of raw heroism, Congress recognized Lewis's mettle on July 16 of that same year with the granting of the gold Lifesaving Medal, First Class. This was followed by Ida's reception of the American Cross of Honor in 1907, only four years before the end of her life. Today, Lime Rock lighthouse still stands, now the private Ida Lewis Yacht Club; and even the U.S. Coast Guard has paid homage to her memory by naming a cutter in Lewis's honor.

In May 1892, Ida Lewis would once again appear on the scene when a group of Fort Adams soldiers was in danger. But this time, one would be beyond her reach.

At nine o'clock on the night of Sunday, May 22, artillerymen William Sheehan, Walter L. Ford, Harry C. Davis, William H. Hathaway and Thomas Moulton were crossing Newport Harbor in Sheehan's sailboat, heading back to the fort from town.[62] The *Newport Daily News* for Monday, May 23, reported, "Every one in the boat was sober, but they evidently were not skilled boatmen." Perhaps the darkness of the night compounded their error. Before the men reached the fort, the boat capsized, pitching all of its occupants into the water. Three of them made for Goat Island: Ford and Moulton reached the safety of the Newport Harbor Light, and Hathaway reached the island's naval torpedo station. That left Davis and Sheehan still in the water. Amid the shouting of the men, the confusion of the darkness and the pull of the waves, the sound of gunfire rang out: it was the indomitable Ida Lewis, firing shots into the air from Lime Rock to let the men know which direction led to safety. One wonders why she didn't row out to them as she'd done so often before. Perhaps she'd seen them too late and knew there was no chance for her to reach them in time, or perhaps she was in the midst of tending the light and couldn't leave her task. Giving them a signal, trying to show them the way, was the best she could do in that moment.

But Sheehan knew he wasn't going to make it. One of his friends—probably Davis—vowed to stay by his side until they were rescued, but Sheehan refused to allow his friend to risk his life. The drowning man warned that if Davis didn't save himself he was sure to go down as well, and "there was no need for two lives to be sacrificed…so he bid him an eternal farewell."

Davis obeyed his companion. Sheehan was pulled to his death by the water, all the while screaming, "Help me! Help me! For God's sake!" But by that time, Davis himself was fighting for his life and couldn't answer his friend's desperate plea.

Meanwhile, a man named Christian Luth had heard the men's cries and launched his skiff from the Newport docks to help them. He found Ford and Moulton first and took them into the small boat, then made for Davis, "who was going down for the last time, and he seized the drowning man by the hair and, with the aid of the other two, pulled him into the boat in an exhausted condition." The three men were then transferred to a fishing schooner, the *Harry and Harvey*, which brought them to the safety of the city's wharves, while the Goat Island torpedo station's launch brought Hathaway in. All four survivors spent the night at the Newport police station under observation for their health and returned to the fort by ambulance the next day. Sheehan's body was recovered and interred in the Fort Adams cemetery.

The harbor was a long way from finished in claiming lives. In June 1898, a body found in the waters of Brenton's Cove proved to be that of forty-three-year-old Private Seeley J. Fitch of Fort Adams' Battery D, a husband and father. It was surmised that he'd tried to take a short cut to the fort on returning from a Sunday afternoon leave, crossing a particular piece of land frequented for just that purpose, "and in descending the steep hill, fell and in falling struck on his head, as there were gashes in the top of his head."[63] No doubt he was knocked out by the fall and drowned while unconscious. Three years later, the *Newport Mercury* reported the drowning death of twenty-one-year-old Private William Holland, "a quiet and sober man…popular with his comrades," whose body was found

The gravestone of the unfortunate William Sheehan in the cemetery at Fort Adams.

Left: The head- and footstones of Private S.J. Fitch and his wife in Fort Adams' cemetery.

Below: The gravestone of Private William Holland in the Fort Adams cemetery.

floating near the fort's dock. Eighteen days earlier, he'd been seen on the fort launch and had subsequently disappeared, leading authorities to determine that he'd fallen overboard.[64]

"His Life Was Sacrificed by Over-Confidence"[65]

But perhaps the most horrifying casualty in Newport Harbor's history was the ghastly, sudden, senseless and, worst of all, preventable accident that in one brutal instant claimed two young lives on August 20, 1881.[66] Though the men involved were navy officers and not Fort Adams soldiers, their harrowing tale took place across the harbor from the fort, and our study of death in the nearby waters would not be complete without it.

Lieutenant Lyman G. Spalding rose that morning with a sense of dread. It was the big day. Admiral Porter was in Newport, and Spalding's torpedo class was scheduled to perform a demonstration of a routine exercise at the torpedo station on Goat Island. The assignment itself was simple enough: row out from the station into the harbor, place a live torpedo, return to the beach and blow the thing up from a safe distance. But Spalding had never been at ease with this kind of work. He couldn't wait until he could graduate with the class of 1881 and his days of being friendly with gunpowder-filled explosive weapons would be over.

Spalding couldn't shake the feeling that something terrible was going to happen that day. As he left his boardinghouse, he wished he was on his way to meet his friends for the sailing excursion he'd been invited to, instead of heading to the station. As it was, he'd had to disappoint them so he could complete this nerve-wracking assignment for his class. At least he had the evening to look forward to—he'd accepted a request to sing at some function, which would be a welcome relief and a chance to relax after the torpedo experiments were over and done with.

On his way out, the lieutenant encountered his landlady Mrs. Ellis and paused. Reaching into his pocket, he pulled out one of his calling cards, bearing his name and home address in Portsmouth, New Hampshire. Handing her the card, he made a startling request: that she keep it on hand so that his comrades would know where to send his body should he not come back.

When Spalding reported for his class, he partnered up for the torpedo exercise with Lieutenant Commander Benjamin L. Edes, widely respected among his comrades as one of the most experienced and knowledgeable men when it came to explosives and electrical firing. When the time came, the two men made all their preparations, careful to observe the proper safety precautions, and rowed the station launch about twenty feet into the harbor to place their torpedo. They did so successfully and returned to the beach, where they attempted to complete the exercise by exploding the weapon. A three-level system of circuits was designed to manage the electrical current that would fire the torpedoes: the first in the electrical room inside the station, the next on the beach and the last on a buoy in the harbor. Breaking the beach connection was one of the precautions trainees took to prevent a torpedo's twenty-five pounds of gunpowder from exploding at a moment that would endanger its handlers. This ensured that the torpedoes would explode only when the connection was reestablished at a safe distance on the shore.

But when Edes and Spalding closed the connection, nothing happened. Their torpedo was a dud.

Captain Selfridge, the torpedo station commander, told the men to fetch another torpedo and try the exercise again. Edes then went inside the station with class instructor Commander Bradford and proceeded to the electrical room, the domain of Lieutenant A.G. Caldwell. When Edes and Bradford entered, Caldwell took no notice of them, his attention focused instead on observing the demonstration going on in the harbor. Nor did Edes try to get Caldwell's attention to inform him of what he was about to do. This was why the lieutenant didn't know that Edes was breaking the connection to his new torpedo, along with the connection for the torpedo of a fellow trainee, Lieutenant Henry L. Manney. This action stopped the flow of electric current to the two torpedoes. All Caldwell saw, after Edes left, were two broken connections—which, as required by his job, he duly closed. By doing so, current to both torpedoes was restored.

Back outside, Commander Bradford told Edes to be sure to break the electrical connection on the beach. This would guarantee that the torpedo could not explode while being placed by the men; it would have to be purposely fired once they reached the safety of the shore. But Edes did not break the beach circuit. He thought the break in the electrical room would serve to prevent current from running to his and Manney's torpedoes. But by now, unbeknownst to Edes, Caldwell had re-closed those connections.

Now, there was nothing to prevent an electrical charge from firing Edes and Spalding's torpedo in the course of the exercise and robbing them of their lives in less than an instant.

Once again, the partners set out into the harbor, Spalding at the oars, the new torpedo lying across Edes's lap. Nearby, their classmate Lieutenant Manney, whose connection Edes had also broken in the electrical room, was engaged in his own attempt at the same exercise with his partner, Master W.H. Slack. Manney called over, "Is the shore connection broken?" to ensure that the electrical current running to the torpedoes was not intact. If that current was flowing, the torpedo would explode before the men could get away.

"I have been ashore and disconnected the wires,"[67] Edes replied. Perhaps he intended that the break in the electrical room would answer Manney's question just as well. None of them were aware that those breaks were no longer in place.

Manney's partner, Slack, felt a twinge of misgiving. He turned to Manney and said that perhaps they had better go ashore to "disconnect our wires from the firing post before we proceed to plant our torpedo."

Edes overheard this. "No need," he countered. "I've disconnected both yours and ours."[68]

As Edes leaned forward in his and Spalding's boat to position the torpedo, Slack caught sight of the electrical connection on the beach—and saw it firmly intact.

Seconds later, a massive concussion rocked the water. When Manney turned to see what had happened, he witnessed a gruesome sight: Spalding and Edes's torpedo had exploded only thirty yards away, blowing both men literally to pieces and sending the remnants of their bodies high into the air above the water. The mangled remains came down in the water along with the detritus of their boat, the shattered pieces of their corpses scattering like broken, discarded toys.

Manney and his partners instantly rowed to the spot, gingerly retrieved what was left of Spalding and returned to shore. Another class boat did the same for Edes.

The words of the *Boston Daily Globe* capture the horror of Edes and Spalding's classmates when the bodies were returned to the station:

> *Men inured to scenes of bloodshed turned away sick on looking at the mangled corpses. One of Edes' legs was blown clear off, both arms were broken, and the face was blackened and disfigured beyond recognition by gunpowder. Lieutenant Spalding's feet were both torn off. The calf of one leg was torn literally into shreds. The bones protruded in a horrible manner; the arms and legs were broken and mangled. His abdomen was torn open,*

> *and the bowels protruded. His face was also blackened, so that it could not be recognized. Spalding in life was a splendid specimen of manhood.*[69]

Spalding was unmarried. Edes was a father of two. His wife, according to the same *Boston Daily Globe* report, was "completely prostrated by the terrible bereavement."

How could such a thing happen? This was a class, not warfare. The environment was as controlled as the subject allowed, and safety measures were taken to prevent accidents as much as could be foreseen. But what can never be predicted are the fatal flaws of the human mind, and in this case, Edes inadvertently brought about his own death, and Spalding's, through a single act of thoughtlessness. The story of Edes and Spalding is the ultimate story of death by human error. Caldwell, who had restored the electrical connections Edes had broken, blamed himself for the tragedy and was inconsolable with guilt. We can only imagine Manney's and Slack's state of mind when they learned that their own connection had also been broken and restored and that, had they not stopped the exercise when they did in order to help Edes and Spalding, they too may have been ripped to shreds by the firing of their own torpedo.

A coroner's inquest was quickly held. Visiting the site, hearing the witness testimony and examining all the evidence, the jury found "that on the 29th day of August, A.D. 1881, at the Torpedo Station, said Benjamin L. Eades [*sic*] and L.D. [*sic*] Spalding came to their deaths from an accidental explosion of a torpedo, and the jurors further find that if the instructions of the institution had been fulfilled the accident could not have occurred, and no blame can be attached to any officer or man at the Torpedo Station."[70]

Edes's remains were sent to Washington, D.C. Mrs. Ellis, Spalding's landlady, was true to her word and made sure that his body went back home to New Hampshire.

Lyman G. Spalding never had the chance to keep his friends' invitation to sail the bay's glorious waters. His voice was never heard at the event where he'd been invited to sing. William Sheehan, inexperienced sailor though he was, acquired a sailboat to enjoy those same waters, and it brought him only death. As beautiful as Newport's waters are, it must always be remembered that for too many unfortunate or unthinking victims, they have been an ornate, sun-gilded tomb.

Chapter 3

Accidental Death

The walls of Fort Adams are an awe-inspiring sight. Solid, dark grey shale and Maine granite loom above approaching visitors, surrounding the vast six-and-a-half acre parade field in a protective embrace. One instinctively feels a sense of safety ensconced within those walls, as if the fort continues its defensive watch over those who enter. In their day, those walls were built to withstand the mightiest barrage of the enemy. Should any hostile warship approach, its cannon fire would deflect harmlessly off Fort Adams' 1,700-yard stone perimeter.[71]

It was the work of thirty-three years—from 1824 to 1857—to build those walls as they're seen today.[72] The United States had learned the hard lesson taught by the Revolution and War of 1812 that poor defenses would one day spell the destruction of the fledgling nation. No such chances would ever be taken again. The Fortifications Board undertook to completely overhaul the United States' coastal defenses by constructing a series of artillery bases all along the country's eastern seaboard. To assist in this endeavor, President James Monroe sought an engineer who could bring the contemporary French expertise in military engineering to the task. The man selected for the job was Simon Bernard, former aide-de-camp to Napoleon Bonaparte. To plan this extensive system of defenses, known as the "Third System" of coastal fortifications, Bernard worked closely with the American lieutenant colonel Joseph G. Totten, who would later become the first chief engineer of the Army Corps of Engineers. Their combined effort included the design of Fort Adams as the most formidable defensive position on the entire East Coast of the young United States, capable of supporting a garrison of 2,400 troops and an artillery complement of 468 cannon. One of the first features to be completed was the outer land defense extending almost a mile to the south of the fort proper, the only direction from which the fort could be approached over land. Paired with the unparalleled firepower of the west curtain's 117 cannons guarding the entrance to Newport Harbor at Narragansett Bay's East Passage, deterring attack from the sea, the land defenses made Fort Adams an impregnable obstacle to any enemy occupation of the harbor and the city of Newport. As combat technology advanced through the years, the fort continually reinvented itself. Near the turn of the twentieth century, when naval guns developed the capacity to rip down Fort Adams' walls, a line of batteries was added to the south, designed to do the job formerly assigned to the great west curtain: to decimate any enemy fleet before it could reach Newport Harbor. Only with the advent of airpower and the corresponding threat of airstrikes in World War I did Fort Adams begin to lose ground in the race of war technology. The fort stood as the command center for coast artillery bases from Long Island Sound to Martha's Vineyard during World War II, but this was its final service. Considered completely obsolete, the last garrison left Fort Adams in 1950.

Occupational Hazards

While Fortress Monroe in Virginia boasts a larger perimeter, no other fortification outside of Europe can rival the vastness and complexity of Fort Adams' land defenses. This area in particular demonstrates that Bernard and especially Totten, who personally supervised the fort's construction from 1825 to 1838, took quite literally every possibility into consideration in their work. As if the fort's design process were a massive, abstract chess game, every tactic of a hypothetical enemy force by land or sea was imagined and forestalled. Evidence of Totten's military genius lies particularly in the elaborate system of countermines within networks of brick and stone tunnels, amounting to a length of approximately 2,500 feet if laid end to end, running through the fort's outer walls. In the event of a land siege, enemy forces would establish their base beyond the range of the fort's artillery and send out specialists called sappers. Their job was to burrow underground from a distance, get close to the foundations of the fort's walls, plant explosives there and bring the walls down. This would accomplish two goals desirable to the enemy: destroy the fort's artillery defenses within the walls and create massive breaches that would

allow the enemy infantry to waltz right in fairly unopposed. Totten's countermines, however, afforded the fort's defenders an opportunity to thwart such devastating attacks. During a siege, defenders would man the brick tunnels to listen closely for any sound that might signal the sappers' approach. Should the men hear those sounds, the defenders would plant their own explosives at the countermines and retreat, collapsing the wall at strategic points that would stop the sappers' advance and leave the wall above intact, along with the artillery within.

In addition, shorter "safe passage" tunnels ran underground across the fort's interior and exterior ditches. If a skirmish were taking place in the ditches and the fort's defenders needed to reinforce

Top: The remains of a countermine in one of the listening tunnels.

Bottom: Steps lead from a listening gallery into an underground tunnel, offering safe passage below the exterior ditch to a rifle gallery in the outworks.

the rifle galleries in the outer walls or to retreat from those galleries back into the fort proper, these tunnels allowed them to do so without being exposed to harm by gunfire and shrapnel. It was the creation of these underground "safe transport" tunnels that proved most problematic for the laborers' safety. When construction began on the new fort in 1824, the engineering technology did not exist, as it does now, to simply build the tunnels through the earth. The soil had to first be completely excavated, then the tunnels were constructed and finally the earth was placed back over the finished tunnels. This process of excavating great amounts of earth caused the deaths of at least two men. The first on record was a forty-year-old Bostonian named John Butler. In August 1825, when construction on the new Fort Adams was going strong, Butler was working on a crew excavating a location for one of the underground tunnels. Without warning, the bank of soil piled up from the digging collapsed and killed Butler instantly.[73]

As the largest construction project on the continent, Fort Adams required a mammoth labor force—more men than the small city of Newport could provide at that time. Lieutenant Colonel Totten wisely took advantage of the depressed economic conditions in Ireland to advertise years of steady work on the labor force at Fort Adams. In response, some five hundred Irishmen brought their families to Newport, and their descendants eventually settled neighborhoods in the fort's vicinity. Today, a drive through the Fifth Ward on the way to Fort Adams reveals house after house adorned with Irish flags—perhaps belonging to descendants of the very same Fort Adams laborers. This was the beginning of Newport's long and proud Irish heritage, as well as an example of the city's tradition of religious diversity. Roman Catholicism had come to Newport's shores during the Revolution with the arrival of Hessian and later French troops, but the religion did not maintain a strong presence thereafter. Despite Newport's long history of free worship for a variety of faiths, Catholics began a prominent and permanent presence in the city for the first time only with the men who built Fort Adams. The first Roman Catholic parish in the state of Rhode Island was begun by the Boston archdiocese in 1828 specifically to serve the hundreds of Irish families whose men were laboring on the fort.[74] After a small beginning, using an adapted building to gather for Mass once a month, the congregation built a larger church dedicated to St. Joseph in 1833. When the Catholic population outgrew even that structure, the neo-Gothic brownstone church officially called the Holy Name of Mary, Our Lady of the Isle (St. Mary's) was constructed on the corner of Spring Street and Memorial Boulevard between 1848 and 1852. The same men who built Fort Adams worked also

St. Mary's Church as it appears today.

to build this house of worship, partially using leftover construction materials from the fort. The presence of this church announced not only the new establishment of an ancient faith but also the fact that the Irish now claimed Newport as their home. In 1953, the church would gain fame as the venue for the wedding of future president John F. Kennedy and his wife, Jacqueline. To this day, a small gold plate marks pew number ten as the favored seat of the ill-fated president when he attended Mass during his summer visits to his in-laws' estate, Hammersmith Farm.

Some of the Irish who had come to Newport seeking a better life than the one they'd known in their homeland found death and suffering in the place of opportunity and prosperity. In March 1827, nearly two years after John Butler had lost his life, Irish laborers John Tracy and Patrick Kennedy were involved in an accident identical to the one that killed Butler.[75] After the two men were buried by a collapsed bank of excavated earth, their comrades frantically worked to dig them out. Kennedy was saved; Tracy was pulled from the earth dead, crushed by the weight of the soil. On two separate occasions in 1836, only a month apart, Irish workers were seriously injured.

The first incident took place on September 9, when a scaffold supporting a stone arch fell and "and nearly crushed" the man working on it.[76] Less than a month later, on October 2, Irishman Michael Quin was engaged in blasting rock—presumably in another attempt at excavating for tunnel construction—when he was somehow caught in one of the explosions. He lost his right arm as a result.[77]

Fallen from the Heights

Today, the underground tunnels that Butler and Tracy sacrificed their lives to create are dangerously unstable and off-limits to visitors. Portions of the listening tunnels, however, remain in good shape even after more than 180 years and are one of the highlights of the Fort Adams tour. But the heights of Fort Adams' shale and granite walls also beckon adventurous visitors. Tour guests will frequently ask, "Can't we go up on top of the walls?" to which the guide answers, always and unequivocally, a firm but civil, "No." Disappointment is visible on the visitor's face as he or she follows up with "Why not?"

The answer is simple. Over the course of the fort's history, no fewer than six people have been killed by falling from the walls of Fort Adams—and those cases are only those that can be discovered through newspaper reports. Quite possibly an even greater, unrecorded number found death by plunging accidentally—or purposely—from those heights.

In 1824, the old Fort Adams was still standing and garrisoned while construction began on the outworks of the new and larger fort. On the second of October in that year, Corporal John Cazy was found dead at the foot of one of the old fort's walls. According to the *Rhode-Island Republican* of October 14, it was "supposed he fell from the heights, in a fit of derangement."[78] This turn of phrase is most intriguing. What exactly is meant by "fit of derangement"? Did Cazy experience some kind of mental or emotional breakdown? Was he suddenly struck with insanity? Did he commit suicide? Perhaps "derangement" means the same as intoxication—did he fall because he was impaired by alcohol or some other substance? We will probably never know the real cause of Cazy's fall, especially since there is no evidence that any of his comrades witnessed the event.

In a very odd occurrence in November 1844, only three years after the new fort was officially garrisoned, three men on duty patrolling the walls all fell at the same time. The *Newport Mercury* of November 16 reported that

Unidentified soldier, early 1900s, reflecting a romantic ideal of Fort Adams' ramparts. *MSG Martin F. Dugan Collection; courtesy of the Fort Adams Trust.*

this was "occasioned by the darkness of the night." Still, how all three could fall at once is rather mysterious. Could there have been a scuffle among the men? Two soldiers suffered injuries; the third, a soldier by the name of James Halsey, was killed on the spot.[79] This was followed in February 1864

The gravestone of James Halsey in Fort Adams' cemetery.

The gravestone of Private Mayo in Fort Adams' cemetery is now barely legible.

by the death of one Private Mayo, who also fell from one of Fort Adams' walls and died from his injuries half an hour later.[80] Given the time of year, it's possible that Mayo might have slipped on ice.

Certainly one of the most tragic deaths resulting from a fall was the 1907 suicide of Private Langdon, whose story was told in Chapter 1. But Langdon's leap from the iron balcony had a chillingly similar prelude in the utterly senseless death of Private Ephraim Lajoie only six months earlier, in September 1906.[81] At approximately 1:00 a.m. on Saturday, September 15, Lajoie, who resided in the brand-new brick upper-story enlisted men's barracks, rose from his bed and sleep-walked out of a window on the interior ditch side, plummeting some forty feet before striking the ground below. Lajoie lingered for a full agonizing day before finally succumbing to his injuries.

Killed in the Line of Duty

Perhaps the most terrible accident to occur in Fort Adams' long history, the only single event to result in multiple deaths, was a fire that took the lives of Privates Harry I. Harris, Fredrick W. Kull, William H. Butler and a fourth unidentified soldier in 1898.[82]

The Spanish-American War was on, and Fort Adams' garrison, though far to the north of the theater of combat, was actively participating in the war, training soldiers and deploying them to the centers of action. At about a quarter to six on the evening of December 19, a lighted kerosene lamp in the loft of one of the fort's horse stables exploded, catching on fire the hay and other feed stored there and setting the whole loft aflame. The instant the guard on duty realized that the stables were burning, he fired his pistol to summon aid. The regiment bugler heard the shot and responded by sounding the fire signal, bringing the whole garrison to a man to the endangered stable. The animals were top priority, and the soldiers worked feverishly yet efficiently to lead all ninety-five horses to safety. When that task was accomplished, the next was, naturally, to save as much material property as possible. The men worked quickly, yet with some measure of confidence: the fire would be confined to the loft for a while, and there was ample time to shift goods away from the stable.

But then, without warning, about half an hour after the fire had started, "a terrific explosion occurred which tore the roof from the building, hurling the timbers in every direction,"[83] blowing out large portions of the brick walls and shooting a column of fire into the sky, bursting overhead like a diabolical firework. The men were utterly shocked—never could they have prepared for this. The only substances in the barn were supposed to be feed and equipment for the horses. No munitions or other explosives were supposed to be anywhere inside or even near this structure of wood and brick, so obviously a potential tinderbox. Yet such a blast could only come from some kind of explosive matter. Some of the men managed to escape on their own power; most were pulled out with burns or with bones broken or crushed by timbers thrown from the loft by the explosion. Even the men outside the building weren't safe from timbers and other debris. At first, in the confusion, it wasn't clear whether any of the men had been killed—the focus had to be on the living who were badly injured by the effects of the explosion. Now, the soldiers had to fight on two fronts: stop the fire, and get their comrades to the infirmary as soon as possible.

Thankfully, they weren't alone for long. Navy men from the Goat Island torpedo station saw the blaze and bravely set out across the harbor in launches to help fight it. Newport police also received word, but Captain Garnett delayed notifying the city's fire station as Fort Adams lay technically outside city limits. He consulted Mayor Patrick Boyle, who told Garnett in no uncertain terms that help not only should but must be sent, and immediately—and in future, Garnett shouldn't wait to ask.

Those who had escaped unscathed and were still able to work turned their attention from fighting the fire to preventing it from spreading, and by doing so they saved the rest of the fort buildings. A civilian neighbor was not so fortunate. Sparks from the stable fire traveled far, some lighting on a barn belonging to a property called the Battey Estate and burning that building to the ground. Luckily, the Battey home was spared with minimal scorch damage.

After a hellish two hours, by the combined efforts of soldiers, sailors and firemen, the inferno was under control, but it had taken with it the whole stable except its brick. It was one of the men from the torpedo station who discovered the first fatality: a charred man lying under a timber, just outside of the stable. He wasn't identified until the next day: twenty-one-year-old Private Harry I. Harris, identifiable only by a ring on his finger and by "the trimmings of the underclothing."[84] About another two hours later, when the barn was considered safe to enter, soldiers discovered what was left of Swiss native Private Frederick W. Kull, twenty-five years of age, pinned under a timber like Harris and "very badly disfigured. The skull was gone, the forearms and lower legs burned away, and the front part of the trunk badly

The graves of Private William H. Butler (left) and Private Frederick W. Kull (right) lie side by side in Fort Adams' cemetery.

burned."[85] The remains of thirty-year-old Private William H. Butler, as well as those of a soldier who remained unidentified even at the men's collective funeral, were not found until the following day.

Kull, Butler and the unknown man were interred in the cemetery at Fort Adams, where they lie side by side to this day, just as they had worked side by side in performing their duty on the night they lost their lives. As Harris had been a member of Touro Synagogue, the earliest synagogue in New England and home to one of the oldest Jewish congregations in America,[86] his remains were transported across the harbor by launch to become the very first burial in Newport's new Jewish cemetery. A military caisson traveled along the road from the fort to meet Harris' casket at the city docks, where Rabbi Baruch was waiting, and the whole procession journeyed from there to the place of interment.

Such was the outrage, the communal anger striving to find direction in the wake of the apparently senseless, pointless loss of four lives—and that not even in combat—that sabotage was immediately suspected. An army

Private Harry I. Harris's gravestone in Newport's Jewish Cemetery is engraved in English and Hebrew and displays both the common and Jewish calendar years.

court of inquiry was held to determine the cause of the fire—and who was responsible for placing explosives in the stable loft. In addition to the plume of flame that only explosives could have caused, survivors reported hearing rapid "popping" sounds from the loft, as of sidearm bullets being set off. Such small ammunition would not account for the power of the main explosion, though, and the *Pawtucket Evening Times* surmised that gunpowder used in "blank" artillery salutes had been stored in the loft by mistake.[87] The quartermaster expressed shock at the whole affair and claimed that he was unaware of any explosive matter being stored near the stable, let alone inside it in defiance of strict army regulations.

On January 13, the *Newport Daily News* reported that, although the inquiry's findings had not yet been made public, there was a strong likelihood that the official verdict would simply be "accident." Harris's death record bears out the Pawtucket newspaper's suggestion that the explosion had been caused by saluting powder, but this begs the question of how the substance got into the stable loft in the first place.

Livestock continued to be an important commodity in the Coast Artillery Corps even as the nation neared the Second World War. On December 24, 1937, thirteen years before Fort Adams closed its gates for the last time, Corporal Abillio Costello, a native of the Açores, suffered a kick from one of the fort's mules.[88] The blow landed him in the Newport Naval Hospital, where he suffered for a full week, undergoing several blood transfusions, before dying of complications from the injury on New Year's Day, 1938.

Death of a Hero

During World War II, Fort Adams stood at the center of artillery defenses stretching along the whole northeast coastline, on high alert in the midst of the Nazi war threat.[89] It wasn't far-fetched or paranoid of Newport to worry about a German assault—with the advance of the U-boat, America's East Coast was more vulnerable than it had been since the War of 1812. Although Newport Harbor no longer possessed the strategic significance of the eighteenth and early nineteenth centuries, it was the home of a large and important naval base that included the United States Naval War College (still based in Newport to this day). Not only were battleships, destroyers, aircraft carriers and all other manner of naval craft stationed here, but the strategies and technology of naval warfare were developed and taught as well. Chiefly to protect this vital center of national defense, Fort Adams' garrison was increased and an anti-submarine net was installed in the waters of Narragansett Bay's East Passage, stretching between Fort Adams and its sister base, Fort Wetherill across the bay at Jamestown. Any Nazi sub attempting to steal past the crossfire of Forts Adams and Wetherill would come up against this innovative device and be unable to approach the naval base itself.

It was during this troubling time that heroes arose to deal with a different threat—an event beyond anyone's control that came not from a foreign enemy, but from a chance of fate.[90] At about 9:30 on the night of July 14, 1941, a small group of Fort Adams soldiers caught sight of a flickering orange glow out in the East Passage. Every man knew that light could mean only one thing: fire. When they ran toward the shoreline to find its source, they saw a thirty-foot power cabin cruiser on the water, nearly engulfed in flame. Worse, the soldiers recognized the cruiser: it belonged to none other than their own quartermaster, Lieutenant George L. Booth. The lieutenant was on board, striving to conquer the flames along with his companion, a Newport woman named Marion Boyle, but it was clear that the two were fighting a losing battle as the fire devoured their vessel. In a matter of moments, the passengers would have to abandon the boat and take their chances in the dark, cold water of the bay—and Marion Boyle couldn't swim.

Without receiving orders, not sparing a second thought—even without stopping to get one of the fort's boats—the seven soldiers on shore leapt into the water and started swimming toward the fire. Privates Robert Murie and David A. Wagner weren't up to the distance or the strong current and had to go back, but Privates William Sharp, Henry Ackers and Walter K. Wilbraham struggled through the half-mile swim and reached the scene. Wilbraham valiantly boarded the cruiser, practically in the midst of the flames. Booth informed Wilbraham that the fire had been caused by an explosion ignited by a leak in one of the engine's gasoline lines and that a second explosion might well be imminent. Immediately, Wilbraham focused his efforts on Marion Boyle, helping her into a life preserver and then into the water, where Ackers and Sharp were waiting. While these two soldiers worked together to support Boyle above the water throughout the long, exhausting swim back to Fort Adams, Wilbraham stayed on the burning vessel to help Booth try to extinguish the fire, and was soon joined by Privates Thomas Sheridan and Robert Fitz-Henry.

Meanwhile, the fire had also been spotted by men at the fort's officers' club as well as some soldiers at Fort Wetherill, and boats were quickly launched from both bases. The four men gratefully boarded the Fort Adams boats while Fort Wetherill's motor mine yawls took over the firefighting. When the blaze was finally quenched, the M-boats towed the embattled cruiser to Fort Adams.

Lieutenant Booth and Marion Boyle were both taken to Fort Adams' infirmary as soon as they arrived on shore. Both were suffering from shock, exposure and burns on their hands and faces from their attempts to try to put out the fire themselves before help arrived. Even so, Miss Boyle's injuries were not serious enough to warrant an overnight stay: a fort ambulance took her back to her own home later that same night. The five soldiers who came to their aid suffered no injuries.

It wasn't long before commendations started rolling in for the seven men whose bravery had made headlines. Even Murie and Wagner, who began the rescue attempt but could not complete it, were included when on July 24, Brigadier General Ralph E. Haines, commander of all Narragansett Bay defenses, officially cited all seven men for their "heroic action in overcoming difficulties of the swift current and cold water of the channel," their willingness to aid others with a "disregard of personal danger" and their "presence of mind" and "quick judgment," all of which had "averted a tragedy" and "reflects great credit upon the entire command."[91] Very likely as a direct result of this honor, twenty-two-year-old Wilbraham was promoted to the rank of corporal the following September.

Exactly six months to the day after his participation in the dramatic rescue at sea, January 14, 1942, Corporal Wilbraham was driving along snow-covered Ruggles Avenue in Newport, along with two fellow soldiers. Private First Class George J. Puskar rode beside Wilbraham, while Private Joseph W. Brown occupied the back seat. It was still early evening, 6:20 p.m., but the truncated daylight of winter had already given way to darkness when Wilbraham lost control of the vehicle. The car skidded on the slippery surface, slewed off the road and spun for fifteen feet before crashing into a tree.

All three men were rushed to the Fort Adams hospital as soon as an ambulance could reach them. Brown escaped with only a broken jaw and some other minor injuries, but Puskar and Wilbraham both suffered fractured skulls. Puskar died that night; Wilbraham fought for his life for two days, but he followed Brown in death at 12:17 a.m. on January 17. Having kept others from tragic death, he was powerless to prevent his own.

On June 11, 1942, five months after Wilbraham's untimely death, the *Newport Daily News* reported that Wilbraham and his six companions in the rescue of Lieutenant Booth and Marion Boyle were awarded the Soldier's Medal, the highest honor given for valor outside of combat. Wilbraham's medal was accepted by his widow.

As in any small town, Fort Adams had its share of fatal accidents throughout its 150 years. It's quite possible that there were many more such incidents than can be recorded here, as indeed is the case with every story in this book. We can be certain only of events that were reported in the newspapers or recorded in public documents. Through carelessness, lack of awareness or simple bad luck, perhaps many more residents or visitors became "permanent additions"[92] to the fort and its surroundings. One such unfortunate visitor was a young woman named Mary Gleason, whose story will deservedly be told in its own chapter.

Chapter 4

The Grip of Death's Hand

Influenza, 1918[93]

Folks called it the "three-day fever": a mild springtime illness blossoming early in 1918 and lasting, as the name implies, for about three days before symptoms cleared. The three-day fever rarely ended in death—it was really just a glorified case of the sniffles, accompanied by a fever that was hardly debilitating. People living in the early twentieth century were accustomed to much more severe illnesses, and they got over the comparatively lightweight three-day fever, as they did so many other minor health annoyances.

Until the illness returned the following fall, with terrible vengeance, in the form of what was called the "Spanish influenza." Its nickname was "the grip"—a colloquial adaptation of the French name for the disease, *la grippe*—and by the time it released its dread grasp on even the furthest limits of the world's population, it would kill more people than had lost their lives on the battlefields of World War I.

Because of their densely concentrated populations, military bases were prime locations for the grip to take hold. On August 28, 1918, influenza made its first appearance at Newport's naval base locations, including the Goat Island torpedo station. It struck swiftly and broadly. Into the early days of September, ambulances ran back and forth from the base stations to the Newport Naval Hospital nonstop throughout the day, struggling to get infected military and civilian personnel to the hospital before the illness had a solid opportunity to spread and reach epidemic status. But no amount of caution, medical knowledge or skill could contain this invisible foe, and in desperation, the navy quickly adopted the only measure left to it: quarantine.

Liberties were heavily monitored, and navy men were forbidden to leave the city except in cases of family emergencies. Visits from family members residing outside of Newport ceased. In what is perhaps a clue to the era's concern with social and class status, the quarantine applied only to enlisted men—for the moment, the movements of officers remained unrestricted.

Modern readers may well shake their heads at some of the suggested prevention measures, wondering how in the world anyone ever thought such actions could prevent illness. Some recommendations sound familiar, such as coughing or sneezing away from others and into a handkerchief, plenty of rest, frequent hand washing and the insistence, later in the epidemic, that public soda fountains use disposable paper cups instead of glasses. Others seem laughable: sitting or lying on the ground was to be avoided, and the First Naval District in Boston hung sheets between patients' beds, confident that these barriers would be sufficient to prevent germs from circulating among patients. No doubt similar treatments were in vogue on other military bases as well, including the Newport naval installations and Fort Adams. Medical professionals strongly advised exposure to fresh air, especially at night, and open-air extensions of hospital wards were constructed. Doctors also suggested that people wear light but warm clothing and be sure to "keep the bowels properly open."[94]

The need for a vaccine was acutely felt as the epidemic reached increasingly frightening proportions. In 1918, doctors and medical researchers knew that illnesses were caused by bacterial or viral infection, and a pneumonia vaccine had been developed. However, the 1918 flu defied all efforts to develop effective vaccines: in the first place, the strain of pneumonia that accompanied the grip in nearly every case had never been seen before; and in the second, researchers were unable to find "the unknown organism causing this disease."[95] Making matters worse, the flu's very origin was misunderstood as the result of a bacterial—not a viral—infection. Despite hopeful announcements that a vaccine had been developed,[96] cooler and more knowledgeable heads correctly insisted that no preventative treatment existed.

On September 15, the quarantine area was allowed to expand beyond the Newport city limits, but navy men were still confined to Aquidneck Island. By that time—only a little more than two weeks after the first reported cases among Newport's naval population—five navy members had died of the grip, and the naval hospital was battling an astronomical 1,050 cases. Compare this to the 6 cases in the city's civilian Newport Hospital, with only one civilian death, and the degree to which military communities suffered in comparison to their civilian neighbors becomes clear. While authorities trumpeted the confident claim that the epidemic was under control in mid-September, the *Newport Daily News* also chillingly—and perhaps prophetically—reported that on September 16, "Fort Adams has only just begun to feel a slight infection."[97] The grip was nowhere near to completing its reign of terror—indeed, it was just warming up.

Calls went out from the navy for nurse volunteers. Women especially responded in great numbers, but by exposing themselves to infected patients and wearing themselves down by working devotedly around the clock to aid the sick, they only added to the numbers affected by the disease, becoming victims themselves. Even as early as mid-September, the situation among the navy was so dire that the Naval Hospital could no longer keep up with the number of influenza cases, despite the addition of a Red Cross building and the former Navy Reserve barracks to the already-existing naval hospital grounds. It wasn't long before "extension hospitals" had to be found. To suit this purpose, the Second Naval District Receiving Barracks were commandeered for use as overflow for the Naval Hospital. In order to facilitate this shift, and to provide the barracks' residents with the treatment of fresh-air conditions then considered vital for treatment of the flu, the men who called those barracks home were ordered to relocate to campground quarters at Oakland Farm in Portsmouth. As they were forced to leave much of their equipment behind, the army garrison at Fort Adams rallied to their aid, providing needed materials and even sending a man to teach the sailors how to adjust to camp living.

The navy contingent made the trip in parade formation, "with flags flying and band playing."[98] During the trek to the campsite, one of the men collapsed, sick with the grip. The very next day, twenty-four men in the Oakland Farm camp fell ill, giving the naval ambulances cause to step up their runs.

By September 17, 12 new influenza cases were reported at Fort Adams. Compared to the burgeoning number among the naval forces—now standing at 1,500 total, with between 100 and 200 new cases arising on a daily basis—the army base was so far escaping practically unscathed, but this luck would not hold out much longer. It was also at this time that the flu was recognized as a true epidemic, with cases starting to flood into Newport Hospital.

As September drew on, the grip appeared to slow down. On September 21, the *Newport Daily News* reported that the number of influenza cases to date rested at 2,726 in the naval district alone. It's important to realize, however, that this was 2,726 cases of flu over a span of *ten days*. The naval hospital alone as of that date was dealing with 2,008 influenza patients, not including the number of flu victims being treated by nursing care in their own homes. The death toll stood at 62 in Newport's navy population alone. Physicians reported responding to as many as 75 new cases in a single day among the civilian population; sometimes entire families were affected—and occasionally, entire families were wiped out completely. But by September 23, the illness appeared to have not only leveled off but also appeared to be decidedly on the wane. Fewer new cases were reported each day. Public health officials expressed enthusiasm about improved weather, claiming that fair conditions would slow and soon stop the momentum of the epidemic.

But the 1918 flu was a deceptive creature. The very next day, the *Newport Daily News* carried the terrible headline "Influenza Increasing" and reported eighty-two total deaths—an increase of twenty in just one day. One hundred thirty-five new cases in the naval population were reported in the morning hours of September 24 alone. Now, civilians began to feel the full force of the disease that had so far concentrated on the military. The proportion of schoolchildren absent with flu stood at 14 percent of Newport's public school students. Beginning September 25, Middletown schools closed completely until further notice. Doctors and nurses were on the verge of physical breakdowns due to constant work. Rather than being in continuous attendance on all afflicted patients, physicians adopted a system of investigating a new case, instructing patients or loved ones as to treatment and departing unless or until the case became urgent. This was intended to conserve time and resources, but one Newport doctor still reported that he had single-handedly responded to two hundred calls in a twenty-four-hour period. Although the Rhode Island Board of Health officially declared influenza to be a reportable disease on September 25, conditions frequently prevented doctors from being able to remember or record every case, leaving perhaps as many as four out of five new cases unreported. With most of the nation's professional nurses called to overseas battlefields, something akin to a "nurse draft" began, in which any and every female citizen who had previously gained any nursing skills whatsoever was "conscripted" to work in hospitals or to care for the sick in private homes. Student nurses also stepped up to supply the increasing need.

Social conditions went from Board of Health recommendations to avoid public gatherings to the outright cancellation of public events and the closure of public places, including theaters, schools and churches. Much of the impetus for such measures came at the request of the public itself. But while these actions may have assisted the public health, they also impacted local businesses in a way that devastated the economy. The war effort suffered, too: men could neither enlist nor qualify for the draft when stricken with influenza. It seemed the nation was being attacked on two fronts: by war in Europe, and by pestilence at home. Even attendance at funerals of those killed by the grip was restricted by the Board of Health, which, though tasked with the handling of this disease, could find little time to gather for discussion and decision since its members, all physicians, were constantly occupied in tending the sick.

The people of Newport, military and civilian alike, were locked in on themselves. The city's streets, once crackling with activity, were lifeless now, its shops vacant, schoolyards empty and silent. Like a medieval village stricken by the Black Plague, Newport became a city of labeled houses: Board of Health signs tacked onto doors and walls warded potential visitors away from homes where a flu victim resided. At one point in late September, Newport was actually in danger of running out of caskets, and more had to be trucked in.

Even as the grip was hammering the civilian population, it began to slacken its hold on the navy, but by September 26, the number of patients at Fort Adams had increased beyond the capacity of the fort's hospital. The YMCA "hut" on fort property was converted into a kind of extension ward.

The epidemic reached its peak in Newport in late September, with 250 new cases reported in a single day. The number of new cases fluctuated from day to day thereafter, but the death count continued to climb from already-contracted cases. Daily death rates numbered in the dozens, putting pressure on undertaking and grave-digging services that were already struggling, as were all businesses, with a depleted labor force. City workers were pressed into service to assist with the creation of new graves. New incidents of the disease, though, were now mild in severity. This was attributed to increased public awareness and the taking of greater precautions.

As the month began, Fort Adams, which had begun showing signs of influenza's presence two weeks before, had already experienced eighty-five cases of the grip or resulting pneumonia and two deaths. As of this writing, the name of the first flu casualty is unknown; the second was Private Hyman Sonkin, who fell to the disease on September 29. On October 6, when the statewide death toll stood at fifty-two persons on that single day, the fort lost a twenty-seven-year-old quartermaster, Sergeant Harold T. Brierley, to the illness. Brierley, born and raised in Newport, had only enlisted the previous spring and hadn't served at Fort Adams a full year.

Lieutenant Byron J. Brown followed on October 9—his death, like Brierley's, resulting from pneumonia after a bout of the grip. Ironically, by that date, the number of new cases was dropping drastically, indicating that

Above: Influenza patients were treated at Fort Adams' hospital, built just south of the fort proper in 1900. *National Archives; acquired courtesy of Daniel P. Titus.*

Left: The grave of baby Geary, daughter of Delia and Lieutenant Richard Geary and victim of the merciless influenza of 1918.

the epidemic had nearly run its course. Still, the closure of public places remained in effect, lest the disease make a comeback by the community's premature return to normal activities.

Private Frederick H. Ogilvie's name was added to the death roll on October 23. By that time, Fort Adams' men could leave the fort's environs but were still prohibited from leaving the city of Newport.

Not until nearly mid-October did the epidemic show a steady plummet. Gradually, bans on travel and public gatherings were lifted, but restrictions remained in place, especially with regard to visiting neighboring cities such as Providence and Fall River, where the illness began later than in Newport and had not yet abated. The epidemic began moving westward but continued clinging to the East Coast in sporadic cases into mid-December before appearing to vanish completely. It managed to make a comeback in the early months of 1919, which health authorities attributed to a hasty lifting of all bans on public events and gatherings. This resurgence of the illness was "severe…with a high mortality" but thankfully "did not last very long."[99] By the time the disease had fully run its course, the state of Rhode Island had seen about 30,000 flu cases and 2,306 deaths;[100] across the whole nation, influenza had taken 675,000 lives.[101]

Though the 1918 flu killed five soldiers at Fort Adams in the space of one month, there is only one grave in the fort's cemetery belonging to a victim of that epidemic, and her story bears witness to just how long the reach of this terrible disease could be. On the fifth of October, Delia Theresa Geary, the twenty-five-year-old wife of native Irishman Lieutenant Richard Geary, was lying in a bed at Newport Hospital, stricken with influenza—and pregnant with a baby girl.[102] The illness, likely accompanied by fever, forced Delia into early labor. Her daughter was born prematurely and died before even being named; Delia followed only moments later. The official record gives the cause of her death as "Broncho Pneumonia; Influenza; Childbirth." The little Geary baby herself did not have influenza, but it killed her nonetheless. She was buried in the cemetery at her father's post; her mother was interred in St. Columba's Catholic Cemetery in Middletown.

It seems there is little comfort to be taken from such massive loss of life, especially when that loss is caused by forces utterly beyond human control. But the victims of the 1918 influenza did not die for nothing: the untimely deaths inflicted by this specific epidemic provided the motivation, for the first time, for the medical community to seriously explore the development of an influenza vaccine.[103] The 1919 report of the secretary of the Rhode Island Board of Health stated that "much diligent work has been done in 1919 by the most able investigators in the world in the endeavor to learn more regarding this terrible malady, but results have not been very gratifying, its cause is not known, and no specific remedy has been found."[104] It would be decades before the creation of a successful inoculation against the flu would answer the secretary's hope that "possibly such a method of treatment may be discovered at some future time and our laboratories under such conditions would promptly prepare and distribute any such serum or vaccine as might be found of service."[105] The flu vaccines available today are the ultimate result of those initial stumbling attempts to prevent such a tragic epidemic from ever occurring again. Though it is tempting to use terms like "senseless" or "meaningless" to describe the more than half a million flu deaths of 1918 and early 1919, those whose lives were cut short by the epidemic in fact left an invaluable legacy by spurring medicine to action through their suffering.

Chapter 5

Cold Case

The Strange Demise of Mary Gleason

The interior ditch is a quiet place, still and peaceful. After the last tour has departed, when silence settles on the fort, the westering sun throws the shadow of the exterior wall across the narrow paved road; beyond the south gate, the bay glistens prism-like in its final glory of the day.

But a glance at the walls reveals the true purpose of this place. More than any other area of Fort Adams, the interior ditch was designed to be a killing zone. It wasn't likely that any hostile force would be able to penetrate the formidable outer defenses—beginning with the southern redoubt, a small fortress in itself one mile south of the fort's outer wall. Even should the redoubt be overrun, no sane commander would order his infantry to take the logical next step of assaulting the fort directly. The only access over land was via the *glacis*, a long, upward-sloping grade of land that, from the start, placed invaders at a disadvantage on low ground while the fort's defenders occupied the more strategic high ground. The remains of the *glacis* can still be seen today, but the presence of a rugby field and navy housing obscures the fact that this slope was originally a wide-open space. This meant that enemy infantry attempting to traverse the *glacis* would be completely exposed to artillery fire from atop the fort's outer walls. Any force approaching over land would be handily eliminated before getting within half a mile of the fort proper. Still, the fort's outer defenses weren't taken for granted in its design. On the very slim chance that enemy troops were able to push through to the exterior wall, they would funnel into the interior ditch and face a line of flank howitzers blasting canister shot through their ranks. Horror stories from the Civil War tell of human beings completely obliterated by canister: as the name implies, a metal cylinder crafted to explode in midair and scatter its contents—musket balls, rusty nails, bits of scrap metal—at high velocity, shearing through bodies as if they were paper dolls. Men could be vaporized by canister, flesh and bone reduced to a pink mist. That was the greeting that awaited any land force that got that close to Fort Adams. If this wasn't enough, a reverse-fire gallery in the exterior wall would loose rifle volleys onto the enemy from behind. Had Fort Adams ever been assaulted, it would have been a literal bloodbath.

Fort Adams' interior ditch never became the gore-filled moat it was intended to be. Still, the ditch has claimed six victims over the years. We have already met five: Cazy, Halsey, Mayo, Langdon and Lajoie. The sixth was a woman—the only woman to have met her death at the fort in such terrible circumstances.

Mary Gleason, an Irish woman who'd immigrated to the States in 1919, was one of hundreds of domestic workers in Newport in 1925. Her employer, Mrs. Mary A. Atkinson, spoke highly of her, and Miss Gleason had a reputation as "a woman of good character." On the afternoon of Monday, January 19, she paid a call to one Marie Shea, a friend and fellow domestic who worked in a different household. Miss Shea invited her friend to spend the evening, but—fatefully—Mary declined. She'd already made plans: she had to be at Fort Adams at eight o'clock that evening, she explained, to meet Private George P. Henderson, with whom she had lately been "keeping company" (to use the contemporary phrase). Mary left Marie at six o'clock.[106]

It was the last time anyone would see her alive.

Later that evening, Mary departed for her appointment in high spirits. She'd packed a light repast for her rendezvous with Henderson: a basket filled with sandwiches, cookies, small cakes and a bag of sugar accompanied by a cooking pan, perhaps for making tea.[107]

The night was bitterly cold when Mary set out. The town of Kingstown, 11.6 miles south of Newport, registered a maximum temperature of twenty-five degrees and a minimum of nine degrees (Fahrenheit) for the night of Mary's outing, making for a mean temp of seventeen.[108] In 1925, there was no temperature index, which would factor in the wind chill, but wind whips across Brenton's Point with a fury unequalled elsewhere in Newport, and if it was so that evening, the air would have been little short of arctic, feeling far below the actual temperature. Mary would have had a fight on her hands simply to reach the fort. Her devotion to Henderson must have been great indeed, for her to travel all the way out to the Point in such dreadful weather.

Mary had arranged to meet Henderson at the fort's fire station, beyond the exterior wall to the south. She'd been to the fort only two times and was still unsure of its rambling, massive layout. In peacetime 1925, there was no need for substantial troop strength and the fort was sparsely populated, so there weren't many men about from whom Mary could seek assistance. Unaided, she made her way as best she could in the general direction of the fire station, finding the interior ditch and struggling up one of the ramps that had been built a hundred years before to allow mules to pull artillery onto the battlements thirty feet above. She was now wandering into an area that was all but abandoned, its usefulness long outlived, the soldiers now being stationed in locales more suited to contemporary military works than a dry moat created for a land assault that had never come and certainly never would. In the darkness and freezing cold, Mary was utterly alone, dreadfully lost, no doubt confused and certainly gripped by panic when she somehow got past the metal rail a full three feet from the edge of the wall, and her foot struck not earth but open space. She fought the fall by scrabbling at the earth as she went over, managing only to tear a hard clod of grass from its roots before the pull of the fall overtook her and she plummeted into the black void of the ditch.[109]

If she screamed, no one heard her voice. Mary was knocked unconscious when she struck the ground thirty feet below, and as the night wore on, snow began to fall.

Mary's disappearance was reported to the police on the morning of Thursday, January 22, by her beau George Henderson—a surprising length of time, given that their appointment had gone unkept for three nights by then. Henderson claimed that he'd telephoned Mrs. Atkinson, Mary's employer, on Monday evening after Mary failed to turn up for their meeting. Henderson later visited Mary's brothers, John, Patrick and Stephen, to ask if they knew where she was. Having no success, a distraught Henderson then went to Boston to inquire of Mary's whereabouts among her Irish cousins. Presumably, the exhaustion of all options finally prompted Henderson to notify the authorities.[110]

Even after the police became aware of the situation, searches for Mary continued in vain. It was not until the afternoon of Sunday, January 25, that her frozen corpse, half-buried by the same lingering snow that had covered her body on the night of her fall, was found by children at play, sledding down the artillery ramp.[111]

The children—surely frightened out of their wits—had the admirable composure to seek and find one of the soldiers, who notified his superior, Lieutenant William S. Lawton, who in turn contacted the Newport police.

Fort Adams' interior ditch, south side. Mary Gleason fell to her death from the exterior wall on the left.

The top of the exterior wall. Mary Gleason probably walked along this very spot before falling—or being pushed.

As had happened in other cases of violent death in the darker periods of Fort Adams' history, a joint investigation between the army and the local police was launched. When authorities arrived to assess the scene and collect the body, they found Mary lying face-down, her purse beneath her, and on the ground nearby the package of food and an apple displaying three bite marks. A blonde wig lay nearby, leaving her salt-and-pepper hair exposed to view. Mary's dead fingers still clutched the blades of grass she'd ripped from the top of the wall—a sign of her last desperate hope for life.[112]

Foul play was immediately suspected. Henderson was arrested that day, taken to the Newport police station and interrogated for the greater part of the afternoon. The following day, an army court of inquiry was convened by Fort Adams' commanding officer Colonel Samuel G. Shartle, accompanied by Major W.H. Allen and Captain Berthold Vogel, and Henderson was transferred to the fort's stockade. The autopsy of Mary's body was scheduled for the same day, but a full week after her death, her remains were still too frozen to allow examination.[113] The next morning, Tuesday, January 27, Medical Examiners William A. Sherman and Charles W. Stewart were finally able to perform the postmortem exam. Their findings ruled out the possibility of murder, concluding definitively that Mary's death had been the result of a tragic accident. Her body bore no marks that would speak of assault, and her stomach was empty—no food, no poison. She'd fallen thirty feet, lost consciousness on impact with the ground and subsequently froze to death while unconscious. Her funeral was duly held at St. Joseph's Roman Catholic Church on Broadway on Wednesday, January 28, and her remains interred at St. Columba's Cemetery in Middletown.[114]

Case closed.

Only, it wasn't.

It was a shocking twist typically seen only in Hollywood films. Just when the medical examiners had entered their verdict of accidental death, Chief Sweeney received the following letter from Private George Carmack[115] Cordy, then residing at the Providence home of his mother and stepfather, Mr. and Mrs. Charles Slack:

> *Providence, R.I.*
> *Chief of Police, Newport, R.I.*
>
> *I threw Mary Gleason over the moat at Fort Adams last Tuesday night. That's all I care to tell at present. I will give myself up to you in a day or two.*

Pvt. George C. Cordy,
Fort Adams.
P.S. At present am A.W.O.L. Have been two weeks.
G.C.C.[116]

Chief Sweeney tracked Cordy to the Slack home on Thursday, January 29, and arrested the private there. The confessed murderer was promptly returned to his post, immediately taken into custody and questioned regarding Mary's death.[117]

Under heated interrogation, Cordy wove a fantastic tale of romance, jealousy and murder. It began the previous summer, 1924, when Cordy became acquainted with Mary Gleason at Newport Beach and the two fell in love. Their romance was short-lived, however, for the instant Mary set eyes on Private George Henderson—and on his shiny new Ford—she dropped Cordy like a white-hot cannonball. Naturally, Cordy swore vengeance. On the night of January 11, he deserted Fort Adams and headed to his parents' Providence home, remaining there until Sunday, January 18, when he decided to end his fugitive status and turn himself in. But when he returned to the fort, he happened to cross paths with none other than Mary Gleason. Knowing that his former sweetheart was on her way to a tryst with his hated rival, he confronted her. "Why don't you say hello?" he teased, but Mary's only response was "that she did not wish to talk to him." An argument ensued, and overcome with the kind of fury only jealousy can birth, Cordy attacked Mary, overpowered her and threw her over the edge of the exterior wall, assuming that the fall to the ground thirty feet below had killed her. Then, instead of continuing his purpose of turning himself in for desertion, he left the fort's premises and headed downtown to the Army & Navy YMCA, where he took a room for the night and remained in hiding until returning to his parents' home at some point. There, he holed up with a fellow AWOL private by the name of McCauley until his arrest on January 29.[118]

Another army court of inquiry was convened at Fort Adams to determine Cordy's guilt. The investigation unearthed a jumble of contradictions and a history of mental disturbance. Cordy's own mother voiced a long-held belief that her son was insane. The man was found to be a chronic deserter, having gone AWOL from no fewer than three prior installations. His military record was "exceptionally bad…for when he was not listed as a deserter he was serving sentences in military prisons." Nor was this his first desertion from Fort Adams: he'd gone AWOL from the same base once before, a little

George Cordy, seated in front, with law officers Inspector Furey, Captain Palmer and Chief Sweeney standing left to right. *Courtesy of the* Newport Daily News.

more than a month prior, on December 8, 1924.[119] One wonders how Cordy managed to avoid a dishonorable discharge long before.

On the afternoon of January 29, when Cordy was transferred from police custody to the authorities at Fort Adams, he was ordered to reenact his steps in killing Mary Gleason. The *Boston Daily Globe* reported that Cordy's movements during the reenactment were confident, that he described Mary's clothing "perfectly and without hesitation" and that the place he identified as the location of Mary's fall was "only about 30 feet from where the body was found." The private was apparently self-possessed, emotionless and lucid. Cordy blundered, however, when he dated the alleged murder on Tuesday, January 20, and when he claimed that snow was already falling when he encountered and killed Mary.[120] The *Globe*, however, dismissed these as minor issues that need not interfere with Cordy's confession. According to that newspaper, although Colonel Shartle and others at Fort Adams harbored doubts, Newport Police Chief Sweeney, along with Providence Police Chief Inspector James Ahern, were convinced of Cordy's guilt and said as much.[121] The *Globe*'s claims stoked the ire of the *Newport Daily News*, which immediately issued a stern rebuke of "certain Boston newspapers, who have made a number of radical statements."[122] Certainly the *Daily News* had the *Globe* in mind when the Newport paper breathlessly protested that Chief Sweeney had never said or implied anything that might suggest his insistence that the case was one of murder.[123]

On fuller investigation, Cordy's confession fell apart.[124] In the first place, Cordy didn't get the date right on any attempt: the *Newport Daily News* and the *Boston Daily Globe* initially reported that he claimed to have killed Mary on Sunday, January 18, but she had certainly been alive when she visited her friend Marie Shea at 6:00 p.m. on Monday, January 19, just prior to her planned rendezvous with Henderson.[125] Then there was the strange fact that Cordy's letter to Sweeney gave Tuesday, January 20, as the date of the murder, and he apparently repeated that date during the reenactment. Witnesses, including Cordy's friend McCauley, corroborated Cordy's presence in the Slack home in Providence on the actual night of Mary's death, January 19, meaning that he could not have also been in Newport to commit Mary's murder on the same night. Neither did Cordy's name appear in the register of the Newport Army & Navy YMCA where he claimed to have stayed. On this testimony, he had to have been far from the site of Mary's murder when it actually occurred. But this alibi was threatened when the *Newport Daily News* of January 30 reported that "the room clerk at the Army and Navy Association, where Cordy says he stopped that night, is prepared to state that he had room 414 there on the night of [Monday] January 19th, and registered under the name of La Chappelle. The room clerk identified the pictures of Cordy as the man who had that room."[126]

In the end, authorities concluded that the hard evidence did not bear out Cordy's confession. Details brushed off in the *Boston Daily Globe*'s coverage were judged more seriously as discrepancies that proved Cordy's incoherence: his incorrect dating, his inaccurate pinpointing of the location where he threw Mary into the ditch, his uncertainty as to whether he'd pushed Mary or whether she'd fallen in their struggle and his inability to say whether she was carrying any packages (which were found with her body, so surely if Cordy had killed her, he would have been aware of them).[127] Then there were the autopsy results, which revealed no marks of grappling with an assailant. When all of the above combined with witnesses' placing Cordy in Providence on the night of Mary's death, the startling statement from his own mother voicing doubts about his sanity and character testimony from fellow soldiers and superiors at Fort Adams, a picture emerged of Cordy as nothing more than a crackpot trying to get his name in the newspapers.[128] This suspicion was cemented when Cordy's aunt testified that he was with her at her home in Newport on Tuesday, January 20, after his return from Providence.[129] In every witness account, Cordy was nowhere near Fort Adams at any time from the eighteenth to the twentieth, removing him far from the scene of Mary's death.

On February 4, the army court of inquiry concluded its case, concurring with the medical examiners' earlier findings: accidental death due to exposure.[130] As of February 5, George Cordy was still in the Fort Adams infirmary, now being investigated not for murder but for madness, while Mary's beau George Henderson had been released immediately upon the closure of the case.[131] No murder trial was ever held, and the sensational case eventually faded from public attention after garnering prominent coverage in newspapers from Boston to New York for ten days running.

But should it have been put to rest so soon? In the parlance of 1940s movie detectives, "things just don't add up." Consider, for example, the partially consumed apple found beside Mary's corpse. Given the other foodstuffs in her packages, the apple would be presumed hers, yet the autopsy reportedly showed no contents in Mary's stomach. Had she been munching on that apple on her way to the fort, her death coming so quickly thereafter would have halted digestion and at least some of the apple would have remained in her stomach. But there was nothing. If Mary didn't take those three bites, who did? Possibly the apple had been dropped by one of the shocked children who'd discovered her body. But could it have belonged to a murderer? These days, DNA testing would analyze saliva remaining in the bite marks, putting the matter to rest easily, but in Mary's time, no such technology existed. Then there's the matter of her getting over or under that guardrail, three feet away from the edge of the wall. The medical examiners stated in their report that she must have stepped over or ducked under the rail, not seeing the edge of the wall in the darkness. This is possible, especially given Mary's unfamiliarity with the fort's layout, but surely on coming up against a rail she would have been more careful in proceeding further. And what of Henderson? Why did he wait three nights to notify police of his sweetheart's failure to keep their meeting? He claimed that he'd spent that time conducting his own investigation, but his account doesn't square with the statement of those he claimed to have contacted. Henderson's story about contacting Mrs. Atkinson and the Gleason brothers turned out to be just that—a story. Where Henderson claimed that he'd telephoned Mrs. Atkinson on the very night of his planned meeting with Mary, Mrs. Atkinson herself stated that she did not hear from the private until the following morning.[132] Contrary to Henderson's account, Mary's brothers hadn't heard from him at all and knew nothing of their sister's disappearance until the police informed them directly, later in the week, after Henderson's alleged trip to Boston.[133] This could, of course, all be put down to Henderson's distressed emotional state and an inability to remember or think clearly in the wake of his beloved's death in such a sudden and horrible manner. After all, Henderson was repeatedly grilled by army interrogators for three days before his eventual release. Under such intense pressure, he surely would have broken down and revealed something incriminating.

But should George Cordy be dismissed after all? His record of habitual desertion may speak for his confession as a way to get out of the army once and for all, but there is the fact of the YMCA clerk's identification of Cordy as having taken a room on the night of Mary's death. Did Cordy's mother lie about his sanity? What mother wouldn't prefer to see her child alive, even in an asylum, than court-martialed and executed for murder? Did Cordy's family and his friend McCauley cover for him, claiming that he was with them when he was really in Newport taking Mary Gleason's life? Was he indeed mentally unstable—but not as a man who invents murder confessions? Was he criminally insane? A psychopath? Was he unhinged enough to kill a woman he coveted? In a chilling side note, as of January 30, one day after his arrest, Cordy was being considered by law enforcement as a candidate for murderer in the case of sixteen-year-old Leon Rose, whose skull was smashed in by a cement block at Newport's Long Wharf on the very night Cordy went AWOL from the fort.[134] In the Rose case, the boy's body had been covered by a heavy fall of snow during the night—a circumstance eerily similar to the fate of Mary's remains.[135]

Perhaps in the end it's as simple as the autopsy stated—accidental death, due to exposure. That alone is terrible enough. But perhaps there's more. Perhaps lingering in that still, peaceful dry moat at the end of the day is an accusation—a cry of justice too long delayed.

If you visit Fort Adams, take a moment when your tour enters the interior ditch to spare a thought for Mary Gleason, who died alone, frightened and cold on a bitter night long ago.

Chapter 6

Do They Still Stand Watch?

Reports of Strange Phenomena at Fort Adams

The cool, crisp air of a late October evening blew lightly across Fort Adams' parade field. The sun had not quite yet gone down, setting both grey granite and green grass aglow with the last of its light. But on this night, the fort would not settle into its customary dark silence once the sun had dipped below the horizon at Jamestown. Quite the opposite.

A lone figure hurried along the paved path that ringed the parade field, following the line of the east wall.[136] The former officers' quarters, long ago reverberating with sounds of human life, now stood barren, their once-elegant plaster walls broken, window frames and doorways standing empty in an orderly line like worn-out soldiers in formation. Lisa Kotlen was early, among the first of the volunteers to arrive. This part of the fort was deserted, the other Fortress of Nightmares volunteers being mostly clustered near the south wall and interior ditch, where the haunted house event was located. There was more than enough time for Lisa to visit the restrooms in the newly restored overnight barracks before getting into costume and take her time preparing for the opening of the gates.

Lisa was looking forward to the night ahead. Her homemade 1860s period dress of voluminous mourning black, coupled with skillfully applied makeup, would transform her into the ghost of a Civil War widow—a fictional past denizen of Fort Adams whose spirit still lingers, bewailing in a sepulchral voice the loss of her husband, killed in action on some long-ago battlefield and left unburied. The creepy character always scared the proverbial daylights out of visitors to Fort Adams' signature Halloween event. So successful was Lisa in spooking people as she roamed along the wait line that some customers were creeped out enough to actually leave before even entering the attraction.

Lisa rounded the corner and headed up the brick walkway into the overnight barracks. This was the only part of the fort that had been restored to serve a purpose other than its original use: the barracks offers two bunk rooms and all the amenities needed to provide a comfortable overnight stay for scout troops and other groups desiring an overnight experience at the fort. During special events like Fortress, the Fort Adams Trust's highly valued volunteers are given the use of the barracks' two spacious, modern restrooms. Lisa headed down the long corridor, past the double doors to the mess hall, and into one of these restrooms.

While in the room, with the door closed, Lisa heard the door to the parade field open and then fall shut, followed by the sound of distinct footsteps on the wooden floor of the hallway just outside the restroom door.

Lisa hadn't been aware that any of her fellow volunteers had followed her, but now she thought that perhaps she'd been mistaken. So she called out politely, "I'll be done soon!" But the footsteps continued, now pacing back and forth impatiently along the hallway.

Someone must really need to get in here! thought Lisa. Standing at the sink, she called out once more, "I'll be done in a minute!" The insistent pacing continued. But as Lisa approached the restroom door, the footfalls began moving away fast, as if the pacer was now running down the hall. Lisa then heard the parade field door open and close again.

Now, Lisa ran down the hall herself, hoping to catch whoever had been waiting for the restroom. She flung open the outside door—

And stared out onto the totally empty parade field.

The field of vision here is a wide-open six and a half acres. If any person had walked out of that barracks door, he or she would certainly have been seen moving across that vast space.

Had Lisa, in getting ready to play a ghost, encountered a genuine spirit?

Sometimes, visitors to Fort Adams will ask if the fort is haunted. Then they will immediately "correct" themselves by saying something along the lines of, "Wait, there were no battles here. So there are no ghosts." Whether there are ghosts or not is something that only personal experience and belief can tell, but surely this book has shown that if it is possible for the spirits of the dead to linger in the realm of the living, Fort Adams' history provides ample opportunity. And whether one accepts the existence of the paranormal or not, there is no denying that many people have claimed to experience things out of the ordinary within the fort—things that can't be easily explained by appeal to rational or logical causes.

Fort Adams employees and volunteers have heard phantom sounds in this hallway outside the restored overnight barracks.

Lisa Kotlen's experience is not an isolated one among volunteers and staff at Fort Adams. Two others have had similar experiences in the same area of the overnight barracks. The first was Civil War reenactor and Fort Adams Trust volunteer Jim Boardman.[137] During the 2012 Fortress of Nightmares, Jim was camping overnight at the fort in true reenactor style, pitching a tent on the parade field to spend the night instead of making the long commute home at such a late hour. Jim was the only person in the whole fort; everyone associated with the Fortress event had departed, and the gates were now securely locked. At one point during the night, Jim went into one of the barracks restrooms and closed the door.

After a moment, he heard a knock.

It couldn't be mistaken for any other sound—the wind toppling something over, the outside door banging in the breeze. In Jim's own words, "It was a clear knock, three times" on the restroom door.

Thinking that at least one Fortress volunteer besides himself was still in the fort after all, Jim called out, "Occupied!" There was no reply, but Jim didn't hear any footsteps moving away. This led him to believe that whoever had knocked on that door was still there, waiting for him to come out. But when Jim exited the room, no one was in the hallway.

Senior tour guide Bill Goetzinger was the third person to report something inexplicable in the overnight barracks.[138] One evening, on arriving very early for an after-hours group tour, Bill entered the fort through the east gate and locked that gate securely behind him. As had been the case when Jim had his experience in the barracks, Bill was completely alone in the fort, and with the gate locked, he was guaranteed to have the place completely to himself until the time came to give the scheduled tour. But while in the barracks restroom with the door closed, Bill heard a sudden, loud *bang!* in the hallway outside. Bill doesn't believe in ghosts and is consequently reluctant to attribute this occurrence to a paranormal cause, but he admittedly could not account for the actual source of this noise. It certainly couldn't have been caused by any human agency, as Bill was the only person in the fort at the time.

Strange occurrences at Fort Adams are not limited to the evening hours. During a regular daytime tour, Bill was standing at the foot of the northeast bastion steps, waiting for his group to descend. When the last guest came down, Bill asked if anyone was behind him, just to be sure he wasn't leaving anyone behind. The gentleman replied that he had seen someone still up on the bastion before he had started down the stairs. But when Bill went up to check, no one was there.

Since 2010, the Rhode Island Paranormal Research Group (TRIPRG) has been the only professional paranormal investigation team conducting an organized study of Fort Adams.[139] TRIPRG's members have reported a wide range of evidence for various kinds of paranormal activity at the fort: everything from physical sensations like being touched or feeling cold spots, to seeing apparitions with the naked eye, to hearing disembodied voices or capturing EVP—electronic voice phenomena, sounds that aren't heard by witnesses at the time but appear only on recordings. TRIPRG has even captured a compelling photograph of what appears to be an apparition in one of the fort's main gunpowder magazines, complete with what appear to be shadowy contours of leg and arm muscle (see photo on page 95). Even though the gunpowder magazines were never converted to living quarters at

Above: This photograph was captured by TRIPRG in one of the fort's gunpowder magazines. It has not been altered in any way. *Courtesy of Maggie Florio/TRIPRG.*

Left: The entrance to the ominous gunpowder magazines (right), where a great deal of spectral activity has been reported.

any time in the fort's history, this area seems to be a hotbed of paranormal energy. TRIPRG secretary Maggie Florio isn't sure why this is the case but suggests that perhaps it has something to do with the materials out of which the fort is made. According to Maggie, stone, being an organic material, may absorb and retain energy, especially if that stone contains any amount of quartz. The stone of Fort Adams' walls may be acting as a kind of organic recording device, storing images and sounds of the past and playing them back from time to time. Is the material and placement of the gunpowder magazines particularly suited to this phenomenon?

TRIPRG's investigations have certainly turned up some strange things in this area. Aside from the anomaly in the photograph, strange voices have been heard on recordings. At least three times, a woman's voice has been captured in recording that had not been audible at the time of the investigation. In one instance, a female voice appears to say, "It was nothing," and in another, "Leave me alone." We have already met at least two women who might have cause to speak the words, "Leave me alone": the unfortunate Ellen Henry, whose husband shot her in a jealous wrath; and Mary Gleason, whose death may not have been accidental. Does this spectral voice belong to one of them? Is it an echo of one of these long-ago tragedies?

Activity is also common in and near the officers' quarters. On one night in particular, while TRIPRG members were setting up for a public ghost hunt, Maggie Florio walked into the overnight barracks mess hall and was startled to see a tall, blue-eyed, silver-haired man standing in the doorway leading into the first bunk room. As the man was dressed in drab-colored work clothes, Maggie naturally thought he was a Fort Adams Trust employee. At least one Trust guide is always on hand during the ghost hunts and accompanies each group as they make their way around the fort, and on occasion guides will even dress in period costume. So it made perfect sense that Maggie thought she was seeing a guide, but because she didn't think any of the guides for that evening had arrived yet, she was quite surprised by this man's presence. "Oh!" she exclaimed. "I'm sorry, I didn't expect anyone to be in here."

Whereupon the man vanished before her eyes.

At that point, Maggie was convinced that she had witnessed the full-bodied apparition of one of the laborers who had lost his life during the fort's construction. After the figure was gone, Maggie had a strong psychic sense of a name: John O'Loughlin. On a later public ghost hunt that took place on August 10, 2012, TRIPRG members reportedly encountered the spirit of a laborer in the former quartermaster's area. One of the guests in the group happened to know the Irish Gaelic language, and when she spoke some phrases aloud in

The "Scarlet Letter Room" in the officer's quarters, another location where visitors and paranormal investigators have claimed to experience spectral activity.

this ancient tongue, the group's K2 meter, which detects paranormal energy by measuring a location's electromagnetic forces, registered a strong response. Many of the Irishmen who built Fort Adams would likely have spoken their native language, in addition to English, after immigrating to the States. Later that same night, after the hunt's guests had departed, Maggie and some other TRIPRG members went back to that spot and Maggie performed a "spirit rescue"—helping a lost or confused spirit to leave this realm of existence and "cross over" to the afterlife where he or she belongs. Maggie claims that this spirit revealed himself in a painful posture, bent nearly double as if some heavy object had fallen on his upper back. This would certainly seem to fit some of the tragic accidents described in this book, particularly the deaths of

John Butler and John Tracy. Was the spirit of one of the Irish laborers who'd been killed on the job trapped at Fort Adams for more than 180 years?

Some of the auditory phenomena experienced and recorded by TRIPRG chillingly connects directly to the real events of Fort Adams' past. In a room dubbed "the *Scarlet Letter* Room" by Trust employees, due to its honor of providing the location for the filming of the 1979 PBS adaptation of Hawthorne's novel, the TRIPRG group clearly heard a voice—not as an EVP, but at the time, by everyone in the room—speak the words "fight" and "shot". Maggie Florio believes that this voice was referring to the "fight" between William Cornell and William Kane, in which the latter was "shot" to death. Does the tormented spirit of Private Kane haunt the spot of his murder? There may be more physical evidence of his presence as well. On occasion, TRIPRG members and others have witnessed bits of gravel tossed through the air by an invisible agency, close to the entrance to the gunpowder magazines at the far northern end of the officers' quarters. Is the ghost of William Kane still tossing that gravel nearly two hundred years after his murder, trying to get our attention—perhaps wondering why his killer was pardoned?

Another voice in the officers' quarters speaks of a different, very specific event. On the very first day that TRIPRG began investigating the fort, the group conducted an EVP session asking if "anyone" was present among them. On reviewing the recordings later, a voice was heard clearly responding:

"Spalding."

When the group member repeated the question and asked for a name, the voice in playback repeated, more insistently:

"Spalding!"

With research, the terrible story of Lieutenant Lyman G. Spalding was revealed. Since that first EVP, TRIPRG has continued to attempt communication with Lieutenant Spalding's spirit, with quite interesting results. The question, though, is why the lieutenant would linger at the fort when he was a navy man and not a member of the artillery garrison at Fort Adams. Perhaps the violence of his unexpected death was such a shock that his departing spirit sought the first refuge it could find. Spalding's spirit certainly wouldn't wish to seek shelter in the nearby torpedo station, the site he so feared even in life. Did his spirit rush across the harbor to the safety of Fort Adams, and does it remain there to this day?

The most touching EVPs are those of children's voices. One particular recording was made when TRIPRG members placed a digital voice recorder on the windowsill of an empty room in the officer's quarters. The recording came back sounding like a playground—dozens of children's voices laughing, playing, chattering away. The last sound on the recording is the voice of what seems to be a young boy calling *"Dad?* Da-*ad!"* Then the voices fade away, and silence takes their place. Little ones comprise the second-largest group of burials in the Fort Adams cemetery, after the soldiers of the garrison, with eighty-one graves belonging to children and babies.[140] Eighty-one children died in this place over the course of 150 years, most of them ushered into an early grave by disease and a notoriously high infant and early-childhood mortality rate prior to the mid-twentieth century. Do the echoes of their happy times still sound within Fort Adams' walls? Visitors have seen the apparition of a young child in the officers' quarters, which families once called home, and a phantom little girl was once spotted in a closet just before the door swung shut.

Occasionally, the phenomena in the officer's quarters will become a bit more personal. Volunteers Lisa Kotlen and Jim Boardman have both reported being touched by invisible hands in the "Palm Tree Room," so called because that area is used to store decorations and props for the Fort Adams Trust's annual tropic-themed fundraiser, the Newport Storm Luau. On one public ghost hunt, Lisa was standing near the front of the group as members of the paranormal investigation team reviewed data on a computer screen. Suddenly, Lisa felt a pressure on her face: the sensation of a fingertip running down her left cheek, "like the coldest ice cube I've ever felt in my life." At the moment, Lisa didn't pay this much attention as she was focused on the computer screen. Only when she turned to leave the room with the rest of the group did she notice that no one had been standing near her. No person could have touched her face, nor could the touch be blamed on a breeze: not only were all the windows on Lisa's *right* side, but a breeze would not have caused the kind of pressure Lisa had felt on her skin.

On another ghost hunt at the fort, Jim Boardman was assigned to one of the tour groups. In the Palm Tree Room, Jim was standing a little apart from the others, near the large pocket door in the midst of the room. While he stood with his back to the corner, he felt a hand placed between his shoulder blades, in the familiar gesture used when someone wants to pass behind a person and gives wordless notice: *"Don't step back, I'm right behind you."* But when Jim turned around, no one was behind him. Returning his attention to the group, he noticed that one of the female guests was looking at her skirt, as if something had happened to her clothing. When Jim told her that he'd been touched by an unseen hand, the woman replied, "So have I!" and explained that she had just felt something tug on her skirt.

Fortress of Nightmares had come around again. One of the tour guides—we'll call her Becky[141]—was scheduled to accompany two of the public ghost hunts with TRIPRG. Anticipating large groups, as this was the last weekend before Halloween, Becky brought her own flashlight along: a mini-Maglite. She'd purchased it the previous summer, wishing to have her own light in the tunnels in order to free up flashlights for the tour guests. On this night, Becky thought that perhaps there might not be enough flashlights to go around and that guests might have to partner up, so when she arrived and parked her car, she remembered to take her own flashlight along. Slipping the light into her jacket pocket and zipping the pocket closed, she was ready to begin the night.

On the first hunt, Sam, the TRIPRG member conducting the group in one of the officers' quarters rooms, said that she'd like to try a flashlight experiment. This consisted of placing an ordinary flashlight in the middle of the floor, asking general questions of any spirit that might be listening and seeing if the spirit was able to communicate by manipulating the flashlight on and off. But there was a technical problem: Sam's flashlight wasn't working for some reason.

Ever the helpful tour guide, Becky offered her own flashlight.

Becky was instructed to twist the flashlight on just enough so that a slight touch would activate the bulb. She did so, and placed the light with her own hands in the center of the wooden floorboards. Everyone in the group then stomped on the floor to see if simple vibration would set the flashlight going. It didn't. The movements of the living were not enough to turn the flashlight on.

Sam asked several questions. But after a few minutes of no activity from the flashlight, it was clear that this session was going to be uneventful. The time came to move on to another location, and Becky picked up her light, turned it all the way off and returned it to her pocket, taking it out only to light especially dark areas on the tour.

The second and final hunt of the evening began right on the heels of the first. Once again, the group headed into the officers' quarters; but this time Sam's flashlight was working. Still, Becky was told that she could also use her light again if she wished. *Sure, why not,* she thought, as she twisted the light only just toward the "on" position and placed it on the floor as before. Once again, test-stomping ensued. Once again, neither of the flashlights responded to these very earthly vibrations.

All was dark from both flashlights for several minutes. In truth, Becky expected things to go much as they had on the first hunt. Becky was, in fact, a believer in the paranormal. She willingly admitted that things sometimes happened in this world that defied rational inquiry. But she also considered herself a healthy skeptic—she first investigated every possible logical explanation, and only when those were exhausted did she consider that the occurrence might be paranormal in nature. She didn't automatically jump to the spirit world as the cause of any and every odd thing.

So Becky wasn't really expecting much from her humble flashlight during this ghost hunt. She had only offered it the first time as a way to help out, and the second time in a spirit of fun.

Sam began telling a few stories of the group members' experiences at the fort over the past three years. After relating a few events, she came to the story of Lieutenant Spalding. She was not addressing Spalding's ghost. She was simply informing the group about the historical occurrence of his death.

She hadn't spoken three sentences before Becky's light flashed on, with a strong, clear beam, in the center of the floor, when no human hand had touched it.

"My God!" Becky cried out—not from fear, but from utter fascination. How was this happening?

Taking this cue, Sam began speaking directly to Spalding's spirit, asking questions and instructing the "ghost" to turn the light on for yes, off for no, and so forth. The light responded according to this pattern for several minutes, occasionally dimming slowly, slowly to yellow, then gradually coming back up to bright white and generally behaving in a very untypical way. It certainly appeared that genuine communication was going on.

Becky racked her brain trying to think of how this might be possible. She'd read online about how some television ghost shows used this flashlight trick and could have rigged the whole thing. Without intending any disrespect to TRIPRG, she couldn't help wondering if that was what was going on here. But wouldn't the flashlight itself have to be rigged? Wouldn't there have to be a sensor or something inside the light? She thought back over the course of the evening and realized that the light had been on her person the entire time. No one else had touched it. She had been the only one to handle it; she had been the one to twist it on and place it on the floor, both times.

Finally, the time came once again to move on. With some uneasiness, Becky retrieved her flashlight. *Maybe the batteries are going dead, or the bulb is about to go,* she thought. So she tested the light for the rest of the evening, as the ghost hunt moved from one spot to the next.

The flashlight was just fine.

This author has no explanation for Becky's experience. Nor can I say whether Fort Adams is haunted or not. I can only say that I hope it isn't.

Fort Adams' cemetery, with the stunning backdrop of Narragansett Bay and Conanicut Island.

I hope that the souls of the men, women and children who lost their lives here are no longer roaming the place of their deaths but are at peace. I hope that whatever mental or emotional anguish caused men to end their own lives is over. I hope that Lieutenant Spalding is free from fear. I hope that the victims of murder have found a justice beyond this world. I hope that Mary Gleason has found warmth. I hope that the only part of them that still lingers is the memory of their stories.

Fort Adams is far from a place where "nothing ever happened." It's not true that there was never a battle here. The battle here was living. In the end, there was no need for an enemy from foreign shores to attack Fort Adams—its inhabitants were their own worst enemies. In many cases, the enemy was nature itself, from invisible microorganisms that decimated the wider city's population, to the raw, uncontestable power of the ancient sea. More than two hundred graves in Fort Adams' cemetery contain stories that were never recorded, are no longer remembered and will never be told. I hope that this book has been able to keep alive the memories of at least some of them, and to make the cold grey walls resound with their voices once again.

Appendix

Chronological Listing of Death Events at Fort Adams

1819 Private William Cornell shoots Private William Kane to death.

1824 Corporal John Cazy dies by falling from Fort Adams' ramparts.

1825 Laborer John Butler is killed in a construction accident.

1826 The body of Oliver Gragg Jr. is discovered in the waters near Fort Adams.

1827 Irish laborer John Tracy is killed in a construction accident while excavating earth for the construction of Fort Adams' tunnel system.

Ladding Luther, Isaac U. Horton, Samuel Aldritch, James Bromley, Joseph Mason and Samuel Hopkins perish in a storm at sea; remains of one body wash ashore at Fort Adams.

1844 James Halsey dies by falling from Fort Adams' ramparts.

1863 Private John Cook drowns while retrieving a Fort Adams barge at Goat Island.

1864 Private Mayo dies by falling from Fort Adams' ramparts.

1871 H.E. Lourie, aka George F. Drake, commits suicide by slitting his own throat.

1874 Prisoner Kerrigan, aka Howard, is shot to death by a guard while attempting to escape from a disciplinary work detail.

1879 Private Franz Koppe is beaten to death.

Artillery bandsman Peter Rice drowns in the waters near Fort Adams.

1881 Navy Lieutenant Commander Benjamin L. Edes and Navy Lieutenant Lyman G. Spalding are killed in an accidental torpedo blast in Newport Harbor.

1886 First Lieutenant James M. Jones shoots himself to death.

First Sergeant Robert Walker shoots himself to death.

1892 Artilleryman William Sheehan drowns in Newport Harbor while attempting to return to Fort Adams in his sailboat.

1898 Private Seeley J. Fitch drowns in the waters near Fort Adams.

Private Peter Gorman commits suicide by slitting his own throat.

Stable fire kills four soldiers: Frederick W. Kull, William H. Butler, Harry I. Harris and one unknown man.

1901 Private John A. Yeager shoots himself to death.

1906 Private Ephraim Lajoie dies by sleepwalking out of a window of the upper-story enlisted men's barracks.

1907 Private Timothy R. Langdon commits suicide by leaping from a window of the upper-story enlisted men's barracks.

1908 Corporal Nelson Henry shoots his wife three times and then shoots himself to death (his wife survives).

1918 Five men of the garrison die of the influenza epidemic at Fort Adams. The newborn daughter of Lieutenant Richard Geary dies as a result of premature birth brought on by her mother's affliction with influenza and is buried in the fort cemetery.

1925 Mary Gleason dies by a fall from Fort Adams' exterior wall and subsequent exposure in frigid weather.

1938 Corporal Abillio Costello dies of complications from a mule's kick.

1942 Corporal Walter K. Wilbraham, previously commended for heroism in a rescue at sea, dies at the Fort Adams hospital after a car crash on a snowy Newport road.

Notes

Chapter 1

1. Both previous quotes are taken from *United States v. Cornell*, 1819, https://law.resource.org.
2. Ibid. Also in Rondina, *Ghosts of New England*; "Haunting Tales From Aquidneck Island," Middletown Patch, October 2012.
3. Rondina, *Ghosts of New England*, 2012; *United States v. Cornell.*
4. *Newport Mercury*, "Melancholy Occurrence," July 10, 1819; *Providence Gazette*, (William Cornell kills William Kane at Fort Adams), July 10, 1819; *Rhode-Island American*, (William Cornell kills William Kane at Fort Adams), July 9, 1819; *Rhode-Island Republican*, (William Cornell kills William Kane at Fort Adams), July 7, 1819.
5. *United States v. Cornell.* See also Duchesneau, "History of Fort Adams."
6. E.g., the cases of Nicholson/Koppe and Mary Gleason, which will be discussed later in this book.
7. All quotes in this paragraph are from *United States v. Cornell.*
8. *Newport Mercury*, "Reprieve," September 16, 1820. In research conducted by Father Robert Hayman at Providence College and given to the Fort Adams Trust by Vin Arnold.
9. Also in Duchesneau, "History of Fort Adams."
10. All following information on the suspected murder of Rebecca Cornell, and on the Cornell family history, is taken from Crane, *Killed Strangely*, 2002, esp. Introduction, 1–7; chapter 1, 8–58. Also in Rondina, "Haunting Tales From Aquidneck Island."

11. Crane, *Killed Strangely*, 2002, 19.
12. Ibid., 54–55. According to Crane, Cornell was probably executed atop Miantonomi Hill, which is now part of Middletown, Rhode Island. Middletown was not established until 1743, so at the time of William Cornell's execution the spot would have been located within Newport's town limits.
13. Ibid., 141–43.
14. Ibid., 105–44.
15. All information and quotes regarding Lourie, aka Drake, are taken from *Newport Mercury*, (H.E. Lourie, aka George Drake, commits suicide), July 29, 1871.
16. All information on the Howard incident is taken from Duchesneau, "History of Fort Adams"; *Newport Daily News*, "Shot," August 7, 1874. Quotes are from "Shot."
17. Ibid.
18. All newspaper accounts render the private's name as "Kopp," but according to military death and burial records, as well as the inscription on his tombstone, this is a misspelling.
19. All information on the murder of Koppe and the proceedings against Nicholson is taken from the following sources: *Batavia Daily Morning News*, "Miscellaneous Telegrams," November 30, 1879; Duchesneau, "History of Fort Adams"; *National Police Gazette*, "The Soldier Murder," December 20, 1879; *Newport Daily News*, "Death of Kopp and Arrest on Suspicion," November 18, 1879; *Newport Daily News*, "Funeral of the Murdered Soldier," November 20, 1879; *Newport Daily News*, "Investigating Kopp's Death," December 4, 1879; *Newport Daily News*, "Local Affairs," December 12, 1879; *Newport Daily News*, "Was It an Accident?," November 17, 1879; *Newport Mercury*, "An Outrage at Fort Adams," November 22, 1879; *New York Sun*, "Atrocious Murder of a Soldier," November 19, 1879; *Providence Evening Bulletin*, "Released," December 12, 1879.
20. The first quote is from *Newport Daily News*, "Was It an Accident?," November 17, 1879. The second is from *Newport Daily News*, "Investigating Kopp's Death," December 4, 1879.
21. Koppe's funeral announcement in the *Newport Daily News* for November 20, 1879, renders "Coal Harbor," but as there is no known Civil War battle of this name, the paper was likely referring to the infamous Cold Harbor.
22. *Newport Daily News*, "Investigating Kopp's Death," December 4, 1879. From the witness testimony of Sergeant John Brown at the preliminary hearing.
23. Ibid.

24. Ibid., from the witness testimony of Sergeant Lane.
25. Ibid., from the witness testimony of Dr. J.F. Hammond.
26. Ibid.
27. Ibid., from the witness testimony of Sergeant Lane.
28. Ibid., from the witness testimony of Dr. J.F. Hammond.
29. Ibid.
30. Several of the newspapers used as sources in this account give Tuesday morning, November 18, as the date of Koppe's death; but this is probably an error due to the fact that Koppe died at night, when (in those days) journalists would not have been made aware of the event, and the fact that Dr. Hammond wished to begin the autopsy on Tuesday morning. His examination was delayed, however, due to the notification of the Newport coroner.
31. The stockade was built as a small redoubt in 1842 and converted to jail cells and a guard room in 1867. After 1920, it was no longer used and a new stockade was built between the east and southeast gates. Today, the original stockade houses the Fort Adams Trust offices and gift shop. The cells are intact and can be visited.
32. *Providence Evening Bulletin*, "Released," December 12, 1879; *Newport Daily News*, "Local Affairs," December 12, 1879.
33. "Register of Death of Regular Army, 1879 (Jul)–1880 (Jul)," 124–25, *U.S., Register of Deaths in the Regular Army, 1870–1889 for Franz Koppe*, Ancestry.com.
34. *Newport Daily News*, "Investigating Kopp's Death," December 4, 1879.
35. All information on Jones is taken from *Newport Daily News*, "Local Notes," January 4, 1886, January 6, 1886; *Newport Mercury*, "Death Preferred to Court Martial," January 2, 1886. Quote is from "Death Preferred to Court Martial."
36. *Newport Daily News*, "Local Notes," January 6, 1886.
37. All information on Walker is taken from *Newport Mercury*, "Suicide of a Soldier," December 25, 1886.
38. All information on Gorman, including quotes, is taken from *Newport Mercury*, "Death and Funeral at Fort Adams," September 3, 1898.
39. All information on Yeager is taken from *Pawtucket Evening Times*, "Private J.A. Yeager Commits Suicide," August 24, 1901.
40. All information on Langdon is taken from *Newport Mercury*, "Suicide at Fort," March 16, 1907; *Pawtucket Evening Times*, "Fort Adams Soldier Attempts Suicide," March 11, 1907. In 1908, another brick second story would be constructed for the same purpose, atop the fort's south wall. The

1906 barracks, from which Langdon jumped to his death, burned down in 1947. The 1908 portion remains to this day. Duchesneau, "History of Fort Adams."

41. *Pawtucket Evening Times*, "Fort Adams Soldier Attempts Suicide," March 11, 1907.

42. Titus and Foley, "Preservation Plan for the Military Cemetery at Fort Adams," 2011.

43. In 1955, the army turned over Fort Adams to the Department of the Navy. The "Eisenhower House," so named because President Dwight D. Eisenhower summered there for two seasons (1958 and 1960) during his term in office, was built in 1873 as the home of Fort Adams' commanding officer. Duchesneau, "History of Fort Adams"; "Eisenhower House," http://www.eisenhowerhouse.com/history/; "Fort Adams State Park (1965)," http//:www.riparks.com/History/HistoryFortAdams.html.

44. All information on the Henry incident is taken from the following sources: *Newport Daily News*, "Funeral of Corporal Henry," January 4, 1909; *Newport Daily News*, "Funeral of Corporal Nelson Henry," January 2, 1909; *Newport Mercury*, "Tragedy at Fort Adams," January 2, 1909; *Pawtucket Evening Times*, "Corp. Heney [*sic*] Shoots His Wife 3 Times," January 1, 1909.

45. *Newport Mercury*, "Tragedy at Fort Adams," January 2, 1909.

46. Ibid.

47. *Newport Daily News*, "Funeral of Corporal Henry," January 2, 1909.

48. Widow's certificate #714113. "U.S., Civil War Pension Index: General Index to Pension Files, 1861–1934 for Nelson Henry." Ancestry.com.

CHAPTER 2

49. This chapter's title is taken from the headline of the *Boston Daily Globe*'s account of the deaths of Lieutenant Commander Edes and Lieutenant Spalding: *Boston Daily Globe*, "Hurried into Eternity," August 30, 1881.

50. "A Journey Through History," http://www.americascup.com/about/history.

51. Following information on the British occupation of Newport, the siege of the city and the Battle of Rhode Island is taken from McBurney, *Rhode Island Campaign*, 2011, especially chapters 1 (1–21) and 24 (70–95). Information on the role of Brenton's Point in the war and the early history of Fort Adams is taken from Duchesneau, "History of Fort Adams"; Theodore L. Gatchel, "Rock on Which the Storm Will Beat."

52. McBurney, *Rhode Island Campaign*, 2011, especially chapters 5–8 (96–195).
53. Duchesneau, "History of Fort Adams."
54. *Rhode-Island Republican* (Body of Oliver Gragg Jr. found in waters near Fort Adams), June 22, 1826.
55. All information in the following three paragraphs is taken from *Newport Mercury* (Body drifts ashore at Fort Adams, likely victim of boating accident previous May 8), June 23, 1827; *Newport Mercury*, "Drowning," May 26, 1827; *Newport Mercury*, "Drowning," June 2, 1827; *Newport Mercury*, "Drowning," June 9, 1827; *Rhode-Island American*, "Drowning," May 25, 1827.
56. Titus and Foley, "Preservation Plan for the Military Cemetery at Fort Adams," 2001.
57. Ibid.
58. Following information and quotes about Cook are taken from *Newport Mercury* (John Cook drowns in Newport Harbor), September 19, 1863.
59. Following information and quotes about Rice are taken from *Newport Daily News*, "Death by Drowning," January 18, 1879; "U.S. Military Burial Registers, 1768–1921 for Franz Koppe," *Record Book of Interments in the Post Cemetery at Fort Adams*, Ancestry.com.
60. Following information on Ida Lewis and her daring rescues of Fort Adams soldiers is taken from Duchesneau, "History of Fort Adams"; Skomal, *Keeper of Lime Rock*, especially 92–99, 113.
61. *Newport Mercury*, "Fatal Accident," October 22, 1842. In research conducted by Father Robert Hayman at Providence College (RI) and given to the Fort Adams Trust by Vin Arnold.
62. Following information and quotes on Sheehan et. al. are taken from *Newport Daily News*, "Drowned in the Harbor," May 23, 1892.
63. *Newport Daily News*, "A Sad Case," June 18, 1898.
64. *Newport Mercury*, "Soldier Drowned," November 30, 1901.
65. Taken from *Boston Daily Globe*, "Hurried into Eternity," August 30, 1881.
66. All following information is taken from *Boston Daily Globe*, "Hurried into Eternity," August 30, 1881; *Boston Evening Transcript*, "Terrible Explosion at Newport," August 30, 1881; *Newport Daily News*, "The Deadly Torpedo," August 30, 1881; *New York Times*, "Blown Up by a Torpedo," August 30, 1881; *New York Times*, "The Explosion at Newport," September 2, 1881.
67. *Newport Daily News*, "The Deadly Torpedo," August 30, 1881.
68. The previous two quotes are paraphrased from *Newport Daily News*, "The Deadly Torpedo," August 30, 1881.
69. *Boston Daily Globe*, "Hurried into Eternity," August 30, 1881.
70. *Newport Daily News*, "The Deadly Torpedo," August 30, 1881.

CHAPTER 3

71. "Fort Adams State Park," http://www.riparks.com/History/HistoryFortAdams.html.
72. All following information on Fort Adams' design and construction is taken from Duchesneau, "History of Fort Adams"; Gatchel, "Rock on Which the Storm Will Beat."
73. *Newport Mercury*, "Distressing Casualty," August 27, 1825.
74. All information on the history of St. Mary's Church is taken from "St. Mary's Church," http://stmarynewport.org/history; "St. Mary's Church," http://www.visitrhodeisland.com/what-to-see/museums/1243/st-marys-church/.
75. *Newport Mercury,* "Casualty," March 3, 1827. Also in Duchesneau, "History of Fort Adams"; research conducted by Father Robert Hayman at Providence College (RI) and given to the Fort Adams Trust by Vin Arnold, 4.
76. *Newport Mercury*, "Accident," September 10, 1836. In Hayman.
77. *Newport Mercury*, "Accident," October 4, 1836. In Hayman.
78. *Rhode-Island Republican*, "Died," October 14, 1824.
79. *Newport Mercury* (James Halsey killed in fall from Fort Adams' wall), November 16, 1844.
80. *Newport Mercury* (Mayo dies in a fall from the fort's wall), February 27, 1864.
81. All information for Lajoie is taken from *Newport Daily News*, "Walked in His Sleep to Death," September 17, 1906.
82. All following information is taken from *Newport Daily News*, "Four Dead," December 20, 1898; *Newport Daily News*, "The Inquiry into the Fort Accident," January 13, 1898; *Newport Daily News*, "With Military Honors," December 21, 1898; *Newport Mercury*, "A Fatal Fire," December 24, 1898; *Pawtucket Evening Times,* "Buried in Debris," December 20, 1898; *Pawtucket Evening Times,* "Why Blew the Stables Up?," December 21, 1898.
83. *Newport Mercury,* "A Fatal Fire," December 24, 1898.
84. *Newport Daily News,* "Four Dead," December 20, 1898. As Harris was Jewish, the "trimmings of the underclothing" may refer to a *tallit katan*, a short, tasseled kind of undershirt worn by devout Jewish men.
85. Ibid.
86. Touro, an orthodox Jewish synagogue, stands as another example of Newport's tradition of religious freedom and is the oldest synagogue building in the United States. Although Congregation Shearith Israel in New York is older, having been founded in 1654, this congregation

has employed several different synagogue buildings throughout its long history. Touro Synagogue, however, built 1759–63, is the original structure for Congregation Yeshuat Israel. President George Washington visited Touro in August 1790 and subsequently sent the congregation a letter now considered one of the earliest statements of religious rights in United States history, in which the first president penned the famous words "To bigotry, no sanction. To persecution, no assistance." Today, Touro Synagogue holds an annual celebration of Washington's letter every August. "Touro Synagogue," http://tourosynagogue.org/index.php/history-learning/synagogue-history.

87. *Pawtucket Evening Times,* "Why Blew the Stables Up?" December 21, 1898.

88. *Newport Daily News*, "Mule's Kick Fatal to Fort Adams Soldier," January 3, 1938.

89. Fort Adams' state of activity was well justified, as Newport was very nearly threatened by the approach of the German U-boat U-853 on May 5, 1945. From Duchesneau, "History of Fort Adams": "Although Admiral Donitz had issued orders for all U-boats to return to base the U-853 either did not receive them or her captain chose to ignore them. At 1740 on May 5th the U-853 sank the *SS Black Point*, an American merchant ship, off of Point Judith. The next day, the U-853 was intercepted by the Navy destroyer escort *USS Atherton* (DE-169) and the patrol frigate *USS Moberly* (PF-63) and sunk by depth charges. All 55 men of the submarine's crew were killed." U-853 remains in the waters off Block Island to this day and is a prime destination for divers.

90. All information for Wilbraham's rescue efforts and subsequent death in a car crash is taken from the following sources: *Newport Daily News*, "Another Soldier Dies from Car Crash," January 17, 1942; *Newport Daily News*, "Fort Adams Soldiers Win Commendation," July 15, 1941; *Newport Daily News*, "Fort Soldier Dies after Auto Crash," January 15, 1942; *Newport Daily News*, "Soldiers Awarded Medals for Heroism," June 11, 1942; *Newport Daily News*, "Soldiers Commended for Rescue Efforts," July 24, 1941; *Newport Daily News*, "Two Have Close Call as Boat Catches Fire," July 15, 1941; "Walter K. Wilbraham," www.dvrbs.com/Monuments/Collingswood/CollsWW2-WalterKWilbraham.htm; "Walter K. Wilbraham," projects.militarytimes.com/citations-medals-awards/recipient.php?recipientid=114335. The fire is also related in Duchesneau, "History of Fort Adams," but Duchesneau's account gives the fire as the cause of Wilbraham's death, which is not supported by available documentation.

91. *Newport Daily News*, "Soldiers Commended for Rescue Efforts," July 24, 1941.

92. For this colorful phrase, I am indebted to the dark humor of Rob McCormack, director of marketing and the visitor experience for the Fort Adams Trust, as well as that of Fort Adams volunteer Lisa Kotlen.

Chapter 4

93. Information in this chapter is taken from the following sources: "The Deadly Virus: The Influenza Epidemic of 1918," http://www.archives.gov/exhibits/influenza-epidemic/; "Epidemic Influenza," *Biennial Report of the State Board of Health of the State of Rhode Island for Two Years Ending December 31, 1919* (1920); *Newport Daily News*, "Another Slight Drop," October 22, 1918; *Newport Daily News*, "Change for the Better," October 4, 1918; *Newport Daily News*, "City Nearly Clear," October 24, 1918; *Newport Daily News*, "Continues to Improve," October 8, 1918; *Newport Daily News*, "The Death Record," October 10, 1918; *Newport Daily News*, "Deaths Numbered 49," October 26, 1918; *Newport Daily News*, "Decline Still Slow," October 16, 1918; *Newport Daily News*, "Decrease in Influenza," September 21, 1918; *Newport Daily News*, "Drop Steady but Slow," October 14, 1918; *Newport Daily News*, "Epidemic in Control," October 23, 1918; *Newport Daily News*, "Epidemic Still On," October 1, 1918; *Newport Daily News*, "Fewer Cases Reported," October 2, 1918; *Newport Daily News*, "Hard to Find Cases," December 12, 1918; *Newport Daily News*, "Influenza Continues," September 18, 1918; *Newport Daily News*, "Influenza Decreasing," December 19, 1918; *Newport Daily News*, "Influenza Increasing," September 24, 1918; *Newport Daily News*, "Influenza Still Drops," October 9, 1918; *Newport Daily News*, "Little Improvement," October 17, 1918; *Newport Daily News*, "Lowest Recent Number," October 5, 1918; *Newport Daily News*, "Marked Improvement," September 19, 1918; *Newport Daily News*, "Middletown," September 25, 1918; *Newport Daily News*, "More New Cases," October 3, 1918; *Newport Daily News*, "Much Influenza About," December 10, 1918; *Newport Daily News*, "No Marked Improvement," September 17, 1918; *Newport Daily News*, "Not Spanish Influenza," September 10, 1918; *Newport Daily News*, "Only 62 New Cases," October 10, 1918; *Newport Daily News*, "Peak Probably Reached," September 30, 1918; *Newport Daily News*, "Probably 250 New Cases," September 29, 1918; *Newport Daily News*, "Public Places Closed," September 26, 1918; *Newport Daily News*, "Quarantine in Force," September 13, 1918; *Newport Daily News*, "Sent To 'Oakland Farm,'" September 16,

1918; *Newport Daily News*, "Slight Decrease Noted," October 21, 1918; *Newport Daily News*, "Spanish Influenza," September 9, 1918; *Newport Daily News*, "Still Many Sick," October 15, 1918; *Newport Daily News*, "Still 'On the Mend,'" October 19, 1918; *Newport Daily News*, "To Close a Week Early," December 14, 1918; *Newport Daily News*, "To Close Public Places," September 25, 1918; *Newport Daily News*, "To Guard against Spread," September 28, 1918; *Newport Daily News*, "Total of 62 Deaths," September 23, 1918; *Newport Daily News*, "Two Less New Cases," October 12, 1918; *Newport Daily News*, "Worst May Be Over," October 7, 1918; *Pawtucket Evening Times*, "Influenza Toll Grows in State," October 1, 1918; *Pawtucket Evening Times*, "Newport Hard Hit by the Influenza," September 26, 1918; *Pawtucket Evening Times*, "Special Hospitals Are Urged at Once," September 26, 1918; *Pawtucket Evening Times*, "Tells of Vaccine to Stop Influenza," October 2, 1918; United States Department of Health and Human Services, "The Great Pandemic: The United States in 1918–1919," http://www.flu.gov/pandemic/history/1918/the_pandemic/fightinginfluenza/index.html.

94. "Epidemic Influenza," *Biennial Report of the State Board of Health of the State of Rhode Island for Two Years Ending December 31, 1919* (1920).
95. Ibid., 30.
96. E.g., as reported in *Pawtucket Evening Times*, "Tells of Vaccine to Stop Influenza," October 2, 1918.
97. *Newport Daily News*, "Sent To 'Oakland Farm,'" September 16, 1918.
98. Ibid.
99. "Epidemic Influenza," *Biennial Report of the State Board of Health of the State of Rhode Island for Two Years Ending December 31, 1919* (1920).
100. Ibid., 29, 30.
101. "The Great Pandemic: The United States in 1918–1919," http://www.flu.gov.pandemic/history/1918/the_pandemic/index.html. "Epidemic Influenza," *Biennial Report of the State Board of Health of the State of Rhode Island for Two Years Ending December 31, 1919* (1920), 26, 29, estimates the total count much lower, at 400,000.
102. The *Newport Daily News*' death notice for Delia Geary and her child reports that Richard Geary was a lieutenant in the U.S. Navy; this was an error, as both the Newport city directory of 1915 and Geary's enlistment records point out. The 1915 directory lists Richard as a sergeant; the apparent discrepancy is easily explained if he was promoted to lieutenant within the next three years. All information on the Geary family is taken from the following sources: *Deaths Registered in the City of Newport, R.I., for the Year Ending December 31st, 1918*, 1919; *Newport Daily News*, "The Death Record," October 7, 1918; *Newport*

Daily News, "Died," October 7, 1918; "U.S. Army, Register of Enlistments, 1798–1914 for Richard Geary," *Register of Enlistments, United States Army*, 1911, 1914, http://interactive.ancestry.com; "U.S. City Directories, 1821–1989 for Richard Geary," *Newport Directory for the Year Ending July 1919*, Ancestry.com; "U.S. City Directories, 1821–1989 for Richard Sergeant Fort Adams Geary," *Newport Directory for the Year Ending 1915*, Ancestry.com. Quote is taken from *Deaths Registered in the City of Newport, R.I.…1918*.

103. "Epidemic Influenza," *Biennial Report of the State Board of Health of the State of Rhode Island for Two Years Ending December 31, 1919* (1920); *Pawtucket Evening Times*, "Tells of Vaccine to Stop Influenza," October 2, 1918.

104. "Epidemic Influenza," *Biennial Report of the State Board of Health of the State of Rhode Island for Two Years Ending December 31, 1919* (1920), 34.

105. Ibid., 30.

Chapter 5

106. All preceding information in this paragraph is taken from *Newport Daily News*, "Accident Conviction Is Steadily Growing," January 28, 1925; *Newport Daily News*, "Indications That Death of Mary Gleason Was Accident," January 26, 1925. See also *Boston Daily Globe*, "Death of Woman in Moat Thought an Accident," January 26, 1925; *Boston Daily Globe*, "Frozen Body Found in Moat," January 26, 1925. Quotes are from "Indications That Death of Mary Gleason Was Accident."

107. *Boston Daily Globe*, "Frozen Body Found in Moat," January 26, 1925; *Newport Daily News*, "Death Due to Exposure, with No Evidence of Foul Play," January 27, 1925; *Newport Daily News*, "Indications That Death of Mary Gleason Was Accident," January 26, 1925. See also *Boston Daily Globe*, "Death of Woman in Moat Thought an Accident," January 26, 1925; *Boston Daily Globe*, "Officers Probe Death of Girl," January 27, 1925.

108. "Official Weather: 02840," http://weathersource.com/.

109. All preceding information in this paragraph is taken from *Boston Daily Globe*, "Officers Probe Death of Girl," January 27, 1925; *Newport Daily News*, "Death Due to Exposure, with No Evidence of Foul Play," January 27, 1925; *Newport Daily News*, "Indications That Death of Mary Gleason Was Accident," January 26, 1925.

110. All information in this and the preceding paragraph is taken from *Newport Daily News*, "Indications That Death of Mary Gleason Was Accident," January 26, 1925. See also *Boston Daily Globe*, "Death of

Woman in Moat Thought an Accident," January 26, 1925; *Boston Daily Globe*, "Frozen Body Found in Moat," January 26, 1925.

111. *Boston Daily Globe*, "Frozen Body Found in Moat," January 26, 1925; *Newport Daily News*, "Indications That Death of Mary Gleason Was Accident," January 26, 1925. See also *Boston Daily Globe*, "Death of Woman in Moat Thought an Accident," January 26, 1925; *Boston Daily Globe*, "Officers Probe Death of Girl," January 27, 1925.

112. All preceding information in this paragraph taken from *Boston Daily Globe*, "Frozen Body Found in Moat," January 26, 1925; *Newport Daily News*, "Indications That Death of Mary Gleason Was Accident," January 26, 1925. See also *Boston Daily Globe*, "Death of Woman in Moat Thought an Accident," January 26, 1925; *Boston Daily Globe*, "Officers Probe Death of Girl," January 27, 1925.

113. *Newport Daily News*, "Indications That Death of Mary Gleason Was Accident," January 26, 1925. See also *Boston Daily Globe*, "Officers Probe Death of Girl," January 27, 1925.

114. All preceding information in this paragraph is taken from *Boston Daily Globe*, "No Foul Play in Miss Mary Gleason's Death," January 27, 1925; *Boston Daily Globe*, "Officers Probe Death of Girl," January 27, 1925; *Newport Daily News*, "Accident Conviction Is Steadily Growing," January 28, 1925; *Newport Daily News*, "Death Due to Exposure, with No Evidence of Foul Play," January 27, 1925.

115. Cordy's middle name was variously spelled as Camack (*Newport Daily News*, "Private George Cordy, Fort Adams Soldier, Confesses Gleason Murder," January 29, 1925), Carmack (*Boston Daily Globe*, "Officials Cast Doubt on Confession of Murder," January 29, 1925), and Cormack (*Boston Daily Globe*, "Confession of Murder Doubted," January 30, 1925).

116. In *Newport Daily News*, "Cordy, Confessed Murderer, Is Held on Charge of Desertion," January 30, 1925. See also *New York Times*, "Soldier at Newport Says He Killed Woman," January 30, 1925. Early reports (*Newport Daily News*, "Private George Cordy, Fort Adams Soldier, Confesses Gleason Murder," January 29, 1925) indicated that Cordy's confession letter had fingered a fellow soldier (*not* Henderson) for the murder. This was found to be inaccurate when the letter was finally released to the public through the newspaper; the inaccuracy was likely due to the erroneous information typical of early reports, which is common even today.

117. All information in this paragraph is taken from *Boston Daily Globe*, "Officials Cast Doubt on Confession of Murder," January 29, 1925;

Newport Daily News, "Private George Cordy, Fort Adams Soldier, Confesses Gleason Murder," January 29, 1925.

118. All preceding information in this paragraph is taken from Ibid.; *Boston Daily Globe*, "Officials Cast Doubt on Confession of Murder," January 29, 1925; *Newport Daily News*, "Private George Cordy, Fort Adams Soldier, Confesses Gleason Murder," January 29, 1925. Quotes are from *Newport Daily News*, "Cordy, Confessed Murderer, Is Held on Charge of Desertion," January 30, 1925.

119. All preceding information in this paragraph is taken from *Boston Daily Globe*, "Cordy Has Had Bad Army Record for Desertions," January 29, 1925; *Boston Daily Globe*, "Cordy Has Had Bad Army Record for Desertions," January 30, 1925; *Boston Daily Globe*, "Officials Cast Doubt on Confession of Murder," January 29, 1925; *Newport Daily News*, "Cordy, Confessed Murderer, Is Held on Charge of Desertion," January 30, 1925; *Newport Daily News*, "Private Cordy Not in Newport on Night of Gleason Murder," January 31, 1925; *Newport Daily News*, "Private George Cordy, Fort Adams Soldier, Confesses Gleason Murder," January 29, 1925. Cordy was said to have deserted five times according to *New York Times*, "Soldier at Newport Says He Killed Woman," January 30, 1925. Quote is from *Boston Daily Globe*, "Cordy Has Had Bad Army Record for Desertions," January 29, 1925.

120. All preceding information in this paragraph is taken from *Boston Daily Globe*, "Cordy Enacts Alleged Struggle with Woman," January 30, 1925.

121. *Boston Daily Globe*, "Cordy at Home Night Girl Died," January 31, 1925; *Boston Daily Globe*, "Cordy Enacts Alleged Struggle with Woman," January 30, 1925.

122. *Newport Daily News*, "Accident Conviction Is Steadily Growing," January 28, 1925.

123. Ibid.

124. Unless otherwise noted, following information to the end of this paragraph is taken from *Boston Daily Globe*, "Confession of Murder Doubted," January 30, 1925); *Boston Daily Globe*, "Officials Cast Doubt on Confession of Murder," January 29, 1925; *Newport Daily News*, "Private Cordy Not in Newport on Night of Gleason Murder," January 31, 1925.

125. *Boston Daily Globe*, "Officials Cast Doubt on Confession of Murder," January 29, 1925; *Newport Daily News*. "Private George Cordy, Fort Adams Soldier, Confesses Gleason Murder," January 29, 1925.

126. All information after note 125 is taken from *Boston Daily Globe*, "Confession of Murder Doubted," January 30, 1925; *Boston Daily Globe*, "Cordy at Home Night Girl Died," January 31, 1925; *Boston Daily Globe*, "Officials Cast Doubt on Confession of Murder," January 29, 1925; *Newport Daily News*, "Army Court Finds Gleason Death Due to Accident, Not Foul Play," February 4,

1925; *Newport Daily News*, "Cordy, Confessed Murderer, Is Held on Charge of Desertion," January 30, 1925; *Newport Daily News*, "Private Cordy Not in Newport on Night of Gleason Murder," January 31, 1925. Quote is from "Cordy, Confessed Murderer, Is Held on Charge of Desertion."

127. *Newport Daily News*, "Cordy, Confessed Murderer, Is Held on Charge of Desertion," January 30, 1925; *Newport Daily News*, "Private Cordy Not in Newport on Night of Gleason Murder," January 31, 1925.

128. *Boston Daily Globe*, "Confession of Murder Doubted," January 30, 1925; *Newport Daily News*, "Army Court Finds Gleason Death Due to Accident, Not Foul Play," February 4, 1925.

129. *Newport Daily News*, "Private Cordy Not in Newport on Night of Gleason Murder," January 31, 1925.

130. *Boston Daily Globe*, "Find Girl's Death Due to Accident," February 5, 1925; *Boston Daily Globe*, "Mary Gleason's Death Accident," February 4, 1925; *Newport Daily News*, "Army Court Finds Gleason Death Due to Accident, Not Foul Play," February 4, 1925.

131. *Boston Daily Globe*, "Find Girl's Death Due to Accident," February 5, 1925; *Newport Daily News*, "Army Court Finds Gleason Death Due to Accident, Not Foul Play," February 4, 1925.

132. *Newport Daily News*, "Indications That Death of Mary Gleason Was Accident," January 26, 1925.

133. Ibid.

134. *Boston Daily Globe*, "Confession of Murder Doubted," January 30; *Boston Daily Globe*, "Cordy Enacts Alleged Struggle with Woman," January 30; *Newport Daily News*, "Cordy, Confessed Murderer, Is Held on Charge of Desertion," January 30, 1925. Leon Rose's murder was initially reported on the front page of the *Newport Daily News*, January 12, 1925. Interestingly, Sherman, one of the medical examiners who presided over Mary Gleason's autopsy, also presided at the Rose autopsy and pronounced Rose's death as the result of foul play.

135. *Newport Daily News*, "Indications That Death of Mary Gleason Was Accident," January 26, 1925.

Chapter 6

136. Lisa Kotlen, telephone interview with the author, March 30, 2013.

137. Jim Boardman, telephone interview with the author, March 30, 2013.

138. Bill Goetzinger, telephone interview with the author, March 30, 2013.

139. All following information on TRIPRG investigations and experiences has been gathered from the personal experience of the author during participation in two of TRIPRG's public ghost hunts and from Maggie Florio, telephone interview with the author, March 11, 2013.
140. Titus and Foley, "Preservation Plan for the Military Cemetery at Fort Adams," 2001.
141. The guide's name has been changed.

Bibliography

Primary Sources

Deaths Registered in the City of Newport, R.I., for the Year Ending December 31st, 1898. State of Rhode Island Death Records.

Deaths Registered in the City of Newport, R.I., for the Year Ending December 31st, 1918. State of Rhode Island Death Records.

"Epidemic Influenza." *Biennial Report of the State Board of Health of the State of Rhode Island for Two Years Ending December 31, 1919* (1920): 25–35.

Newport Daily News. "Accident Conviction Is Steadily Growing." January 28, 1925.

———. "Another Slight Drop." October 22, 1918.

———. "Another Soldier Dies from Car Crash." January 17, 1942.

———. "Army Court Finds Gleason Death Due to Accident, Not Foul Play." February 4, 1925.

———. "Change for the Better." October 4, 1918.

———. "City Nearly Clear." October 24, 1918.

———. "Continues to Improve." October 8, 1918.
———. "Cordy, Confessed Murderer, Is Held on Charge of Desertion." January 30, 1925.
———. "The Deadly Torpedo." August 30, 1881.
———. "Death by Drowning." January 18, 1879.
———. "Death Due to Exposure, with No Evidence of Foul Play." January 27, 1925.
———. "Death of Kopp and Arrest on Suspicion." November 18, 1879.
———. "The Death Record." October 7, 1918, October 10, 1918.
———. "Deaths Numbered 49." October 26, 1918.
———. "Decline Still Slow." October 16, 1918.
———. "Decrease in Influenza." September 21, 1918.
———. "Died." September 30, 1918, October 7, 1918.
———. "Drop Steady but Slow." October 14, 1918.
———. "Drowned in the Harbor." May 23, 1892.
———. "Epidemic in Control." October 23, 1918.
———. "Epidemic Still On." October 1, 1918.
———. "Fewer Cases Reported." October 2, 1918.
———. "Fort Adams Soldiers Win Commendation." July 15, 1941.
———. "Fort Soldier Dies after Auto Crash." January 15, 1942.
———. "Four Dead." December 20, 1898.
———. "Funeral of Corporal Henry." January 4, 1909.
———. "Funeral of Corporal Nelson Henry." January 2, 1909.
———. "Funeral of the Murdered Soldier." November 20, 1879.
———. "Hard to Find Cases." December 12, 1918.
———. "Indications That Death of Mary Gleason Was Accident." January 26, 1925.
———. "Influenza Continues." September 18, 1918.
———. "Influenza Decreasing." December 19, 1918.
———. "Influenza Increasing." September 24, 1918.
———. "Influenza Still Drops." October 9, 1918.
———. "The Inquiry into the Fort Accident." January 13, 1898.
———. "Investigating Kopp's Death." December 4, 1879.
———. "Little Improvement." October 17, 1918.
———. "Local Affairs." December 12, 1879; January 4, 1886; January 6, 1886.
———. "Local Notes." January 4, 1886; January 6, 1886.
———. "Lowest Recent Number." October 5, 1918.
———. "Marked Improvement." September 19, 1918.
———. "Middletown." September 25, 1918.

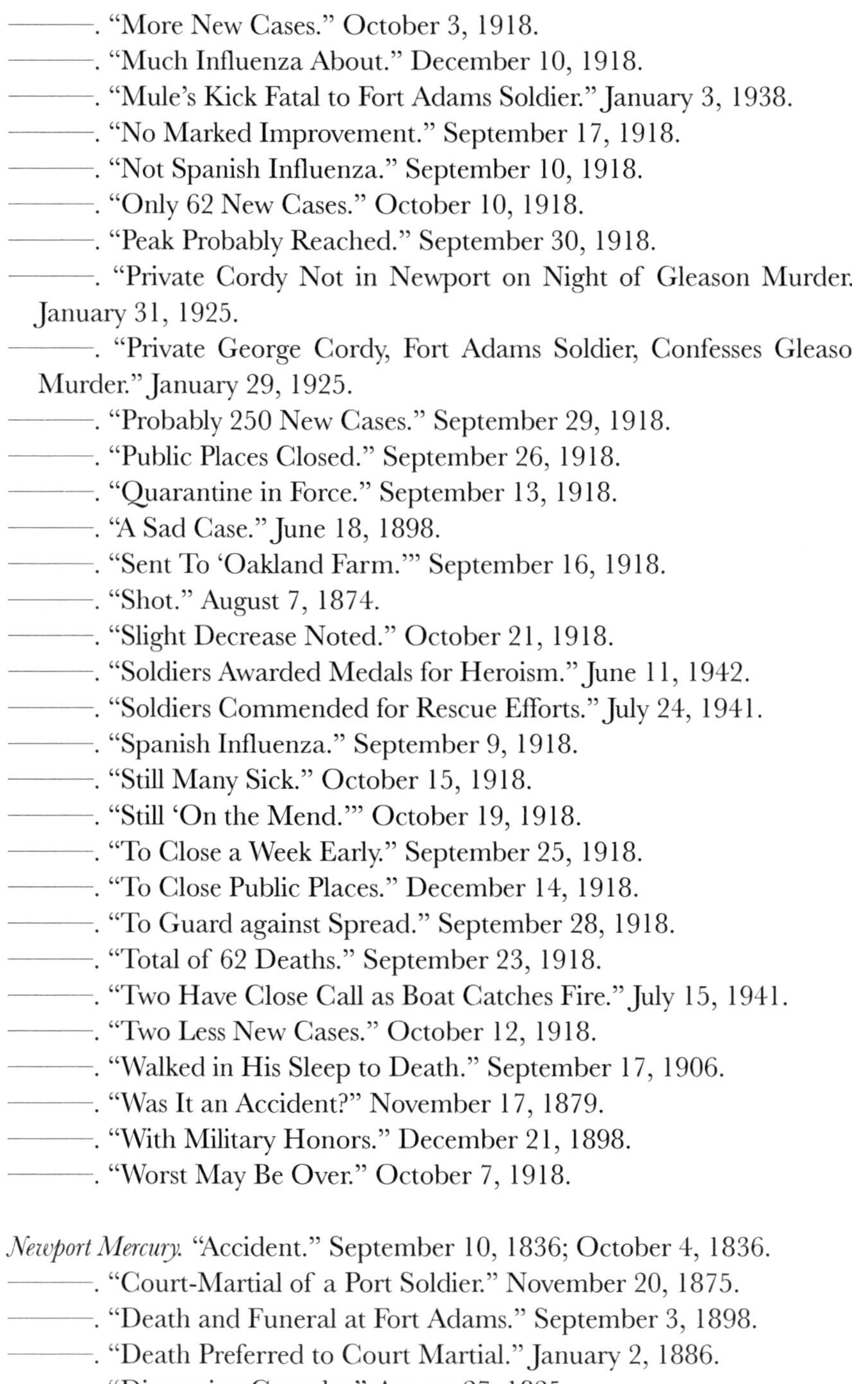

———. "More New Cases." October 3, 1918.
———. "Much Influenza About." December 10, 1918.
———. "Mule's Kick Fatal to Fort Adams Soldier." January 3, 1938.
———. "No Marked Improvement." September 17, 1918.
———. "Not Spanish Influenza." September 10, 1918.
———. "Only 62 New Cases." October 10, 1918.
———. "Peak Probably Reached." September 30, 1918.
———. "Private Cordy Not in Newport on Night of Gleason Murder." January 31, 1925.
———. "Private George Cordy, Fort Adams Soldier, Confesses Gleason Murder." January 29, 1925.
———. "Probably 250 New Cases." September 29, 1918.
———. "Public Places Closed." September 26, 1918.
———. "Quarantine in Force." September 13, 1918.
———. "A Sad Case." June 18, 1898.
———. "Sent To 'Oakland Farm.'" September 16, 1918.
———. "Shot." August 7, 1874.
———. "Slight Decrease Noted." October 21, 1918.
———. "Soldiers Awarded Medals for Heroism." June 11, 1942.
———. "Soldiers Commended for Rescue Efforts." July 24, 1941.
———. "Spanish Influenza." September 9, 1918.
———. "Still Many Sick." October 15, 1918.
———. "Still 'On the Mend.'" October 19, 1918.
———. "To Close a Week Early." September 25, 1918.
———. "To Close Public Places." December 14, 1918.
———. "To Guard against Spread." September 28, 1918.
———. "Total of 62 Deaths." September 23, 1918.
———. "Two Have Close Call as Boat Catches Fire." July 15, 1941.
———. "Two Less New Cases." October 12, 1918.
———. "Walked in His Sleep to Death." September 17, 1906.
———. "Was It an Accident?" November 17, 1879.
———. "With Military Honors." December 21, 1898.
———. "Worst May Be Over." October 7, 1918.

Newport Mercury. "Accident." September 10, 1836; October 4, 1836.
———. "Court-Martial of a Port Soldier." November 20, 1875.
———. "Death and Funeral at Fort Adams." September 3, 1898.
———. "Death Preferred to Court Martial." January 2, 1886.
———. "Distressing Casualty." August 27, 1825.

———. "Fatal Accident." October 22, 1842.
———. "A Fatal Fire." December 24, 1898.
———. (H.E. Lourie, aka George Drake, commits suicide.) July 29, 1871.
———. (John Cook drowns in Newport Harbor.) September 19, 1863.
———. (Mayo dies in a fall from the fort's wall.) February 27, 1864.
———. "An Outrage at Fort Adams." November 22, 1879.
———. "Reprieve." September 16, 1820.
———. "Soldier Drowned." November 30, 1901.
———. "Suicide at Fort." March 16, 1907.
———. "Suicide of a Soldier." December 25, 1886.
———. "Tragedy at Fort Adams." January 2, 1909.

Providence Evening Bulletin. "Released." December 12, 1879.

"Station Hospital." *Inventory of Federal Archives in the States.* Series IV: The Department of War, #38. Providence, RI: Survey of Federal Archives, Division of Women's and Professional Projects, Works Progress Administration, 1938.

Secondary Sources

Crane, Elaine Forman. *Killed Strangely: The Death of Rebecca Cornell.* Ithaca, NY: Cornell University Press, 2002.

Gatchel, Theodore L. "The Rock on Which the Storm Will Beat: Fort Adams and the Defenses of Narragansett Bay." *Newport History* 67, no. 230 (1995): 1–35.

Hayman, Father Robert. Personal research. Providence College, Providence, RI.

McBurney, Christian M. *The Rhode Island Campaign: The First French and American Operation in the Revolutionary War*. Yardley, PA: Westholme, 2011.

Rondina, Christopher. *Ghosts of New England.* On Cape Publications, 2012 (unpublished).

Skomal, Lenore. *The Keeper of Lime Rock: The Remarkable True Story of Ida Lewis, America's Most Celebrated Lighthouse Keeper*. Philadelphia: Running Press, 2002.

Tour Guide Script. Fort Adams Trust, 2013.

Websites and Articles/Documents in Online Databases

Artillery Company of Newport Homepage. Artillery Company of Newport. 2013. http://newportartillery.org/.

"Atrocious Murder of a Soldier." *New York Sun*. November 19, 1879. Old Fulton NY Post Cards. http://fultonhistory.com (accessed March 17, 2013).

"Blown Up by a Torpedo." *New York Times*, August 30, 1881. *New York Times*. http://query.nytimes.com/mem/archive-free/pdf?res=FB0C1FF83E5F15738DDDA90B94D0405B8184F0D3 (accessed May 4, 2013).

(Body drifts ashore at Fort Adams, likely victim of boating accident previous May 8.) *Newport Mercury*, June 23, 1827. America's Historical Newspapers. NewsBank/American Antiquarian Society. 2004. http://docs.newsbank.com/s/HistArchive/ahnpdoc/EANX/1070475826661400/6F20C08F28B84AC5B3E9F27DD72202C7 (accessed February 22, 2013).

(Body of Oliver Gragg Jr. found in waters near Fort Adams.) *Rhode-Island Republican*, June 22, 1826. America's Historical Newspapers. NewsBank/American Antiquarian Society. 2004. http://docs/newsbank.com/s/HistArchive/ahnpdoc/EANX/10E6A1549F71CA18/6F20C08F28B84AC5B3E9F27DD72202C7 (accessed February 22, 2013).

"Buried in Debris." *Pawtucket Evening Times*, December 20, 1898. America's Historical Newspapers. NewsBank/American Antiquarian Society. 2004. http://docs.newsbank.com/s/HistArchive/ahnpdoc/EANX/11F72C3013F13D68/6F20C08F28B84AC5B3E9F27DD72202C7 (accessed April 4, 2013).

"Casualty." *Newport Mercury*, March 3, 1827. America's Historical Newspapers. NewsBank/American Antiquarian Society. 2004. http://docs.newsbank.com/s/HistArchive/ahnpdoc/EANX/1070466F38517EE8/6F20C08F28B84AC5B3E9F27DD72202C7 (accessed April 4, 2013).

"Confession of Murder Doubted." *Boston Daily Globe*, January 30, 1925. ProQuest Historical Newspapers. http://pqasb.pqarchiver.com/boston/access/1879904862.html?FMT=AI&FMTS=ABS:AI&type=historic&date=Jan+30%2C+1925&author=Special+Dispatch+to+the+Globe&pub=Boston+Daily+Globe+%281923-1927%29&edition=&startpage=2&desc=CONFESSION+OF+MURDER+DOUBTED (accessed February 20, 2013).

"Cordy at Home Night Girl Died." *Boston Daily Globe*, January 31, 1925. ProQuest Historical Newspapers. http://pqasb.pqarchiver.com/boston/access/1879916512.html?FMT=AI&FMTS=CITE:AI&type=historic&date=Jan+31%2C+1925&author=&pub=Boston+Daily+Globe+%281923-1927%29&edition=&startpage=18&desc=WOMAN+LEAPS+TO+ICE+60+FEET+UNDER+SPAN (accessed February 20, 2013).

"Cordy Enacts Alleged Struggle with Woman." *Boston Daily Globe*, January 30, 1925. ProQuest Historical Newspapers. http://pqasb.pqarchiver.com/boston/access/1879904872.html?FMT=AI&FMTS=ABS:AI&type=historic&date=Jan+30%2C+1925&author=&pub=Boston+Daily+Globe+%281923-1927%29&edition=&startpage=2&desc=CORDY+ENACTS+ALLEGED+STRUGGLE+WITH+WOMAN (accessed February 20, 2013).

"Cordy Has Had Bad Army Record for Desertions." *Boston Daily Globe*, January 29, 1925. ProQuest Historical Newspapers. http://pqasb.pqarchiver.com/boston/access/1879901072.html?FMT=AI&FMTS=ABS:AI&type=historic&date=Jan+29%2C+1925&author=&pub=Boston+Daily+Globe+%281923-1927%29&edition=&startpage=A1&desc=OFFICIALS+CAST+DOUBT+ON+CONFESSION+OF+MURDER (accessed February 20, 2013).

"Cordy Has Had Bad Army Record for Desertions." *Boston Daily Globe*, January 30, 1925. ProQuest Historical Newspapers. http://pqasb.pqarchiver.

com/boston/access/1879904882.html?FMT=AI&FMTS=CITE:AI&type=historic&date=Jan+30%2C+1925&author=&pub=Boston+Daily+Globe+%281923-1927%29&edition=&startpage=2&desc=CORDY+HAS+HAD+BAD+ARMY+RECORD+FOR+DESERTIONS (accessed February 20, 2013).

"Corp. Heney [*sic*] Shoots His Wife 3 Times." *Pawtucket Evening Times*, January 1, 1909. America's Historical Newspapers. NewsBank/American Antiquarian Society. 2004. http://docs.newsbank.com/s/HistArchive/ahnpdoc/EANX/11FF92469248C170/6F20C08F28B84AC5B3E9F27DD72202C7 (accessed April 4, 2013).

"The Deadly Virus: The Influenza Epidemic of 1918." National Archives and Records Administration. http://www.archives.gov/exhibits/influenza-epidemic/ (accessed April 28, 2013).

"Death of Woman in Moat Thought an Accident." *Boston Daily Globe*, January 26, 1925. ProQuest Historical Newspapers. https://secure.pqarchiver.com/boston/access/1879879742.html?FMT=AI&FMTS=ABS:AI&type=historic&date=Jan+26%2C+1925&author=&pub=Boston+Daily+Globe+%281923-1927%29&edition=&startpage=A1&desc=DEATH+OF+WOMAN+IN+MOAT+THOUGHT+AN+ACCIDENT (accessed February 20, 2013).

"Died." *Rhode-Island Republican*, October 14, 1824. America's Historical Newspapers. NewsBank/American Antiquarian Society. 2004. http://docs.newsbank.com/s/HistArchive/ahnpdoc/EANX/10E58BC76FF1AA98/6F20C08F28B84AC5B3E9F27DD72202C7 (accessed February 19, 2013).

"Drowning." *Newport Mercury*, May 26, 1827. America's Historical Newspapers. NewsBank/American Antiquarian Society. 2004. http://docs.newsbank.com/.

"Drowning." *Newport Mercury*, June 2, 1827. America's Historical Newspapers. NewsBank/American Antiquarian Society. 2004. http://docs.newsbank.com/s/HistArchive/ahnpdoc/EANX/1070474236E0C848/6F20C08F28B84AC5B3E9F27DD72202C7 (accessed February 22, 2013).

"Drowning." *Newport Mercury*, June 9, 1827. America's Historical Newspapers. NewsBank/American Antiquarian Society. 2004. http://docs.newsbank.com/s/HistArchive/ahnpdoc/EANX/1070474DD3619BE0/6F20C08F28B84AC5B3E9F27DD72202C7 (accessed February 22, 2013).

"Drowning." *Rhode-Island American*, May 25, 1827. America's Historical Newspapers. NewsBank/American Antiquarian Society. 2004. http://docs.newsbank.com/s/HistArchive/ahnpdoc/EANX/10E587F6E5323398/6F20C08F28B84AC5B3E9F27DD72202C7 (accessed February 22, 2013).

Duchesneau, John T. "The History of Fort Adams: The Rock on Which the Storm Will Beat." 2007. www.oocities.org/~jmgould/adamshist.html (accessed March 9, 2013).

"Eisenhower House." RI.gov. http://www.eisenhowerhouse.com/history/ (accessed March 31, 2013).

"The Explosion at Newport." *New York Times*, September 2, 1881. http://query.nytimes.com/gst/abstract.html?res=F00915FC3D5E1A738DDDAB0894D1405B8184F0D3 (accessed May 4, 2013).

"Find Girl's Death Due to Accident." *Boston Daily Globe*, February 5, 1925. ProQuest Historical Newspapers. http://pqasb.pqarchiver.com/boston/access/1879942002.html?FMT=AI&FMTS=CITE:AI&type=historic&date=Feb+5%2C+1925&author=&pub=Boston+Daily+Globe+%281923-1927%29&edition=&startpage=6&desc=FIND+GIRL%27S+DEATH+DUE+TO+ACCIDENT (accessed February 20, 2013).

"Fort Adams Soldier Attempts Suicide." *Pawtucket Evening Times*, March 11, 1907. America's Historical Newspapers. NewsBank/American Antiquarian Society. 2004. http://docs.newsbank.com/s/HistArchive/ahnpdoc/EANX/11FF9041C71D9820/6F20C08F28B84AC5B3E9F27DD72202C7 (accessed April 4, 2013).

"Fort Adams State Park (1965)." State of Rhode Island Division of Parks & Recreation. 2012. http://www.riparks.com/History/HistoryFortAdams.html (accessed March 31, 2013).

"Frozen Body Found in Moat." *Boston Daily Globe*, January 26, 1925. ProQuest Historical Newspapers. http://pqasb.pqarchiver.com/boston/access/1879877972.html?FMT=AI&FMTS=CITE:AI&type=historic&date=Jan+26%2C+1925&author=&pub=Boston+Daily+Globe+%281923-1927%29&edition=&startpage=11&desc=FROZEN+BODY+FOUND+IN+MOAT (accessed February 20, 2013).

"The Great Pandemic: The United States in 1918–1919." United States Department of Health and Human Services. http://www.flu.gov/pandemic/history/1918/the_pandemic/fightinginfluenza/index.html; http://www.flu.gov/pandemic/history/1918/the_pandemic/index.html (accessed April 28, 2013).

"Haunting Tales from Aquidneck Island." Middletown Patch. October, 2010. http://middletown.patch.com/articles/aquidneck-islands-haunting-tales (accessed April 28, 2013).

"Hurried into Eternity." *Boston Daily Globe*, August 30, 1881. ProQuest Historical Newspapers. https://secure.pqarchiver.com/boston/access/557991702.html?FMT=AI&FMTS=ABS:AI&type=historic&date=Aug+30%2C+1881&author=Special+Despatch+to+The+Boston+Globe&pub=Boston+Daily+Globe+%281872-1922%29&desc=HURRIED+INTO+ETERNITY (accessed April 4, 2013).

"Influenza Toll Grows in State." *Pawtucket Evening Times*, October 1, 1918. America's Historical Newspapers. NewsBank/American Antiquarian Society. 2004. http://docs.newsbank.com/s/HistArchive/ahnpdoc/EANX/120139CE0A92FC48/6F20C08F28B84AC5B3E9F27DD72202C7 (accessed April 4, 2013).

(James Halsey killed in fall from Fort Adams' wall.) *Newport Mercury*, November 16, 1844. America's Historical Newspapers. NewsBank/American Antiquarian Society. 2004. http://docs.newsbank.com/s/HistArchive/ahnpdoc/EANX/10FF4945F66A30E8/6F20C08F28B84AC5B3E9F27DD72202C7 (accessed February 22, 2013).

"A Journey Through History." America's Cup Event Authority, LLC. 2012–2013. http://www.americascup.com/about/history. (accessed March 4, 2013).

"Mary Gleason's Death Accident." *Boston Daily Globe*, February 4, 1925. ProQuest Historical Newspapers. http://pqasb.pqarchiver.com/boston/access/1879941272.html?FMT=AI&FMTS=CITE:AI&type=historic&date=Feb+4%2C+1925&author=&pub=Boston+Daily+Globe+%281923-1927%29&edition=&startpage=A24&desc=MARY+GLEASON%27S+DEATH+ACCIDENT (accessed February 20, 2013).

"Melancholy Occurrence." *Newport Mercury*, July 10, 1819. America's Historical Newspapers. NewsBank/American Antiquarian Society. 2004. http://docs.newsbank.com/s/HistArchive/ahnpdoc/EANX/10703C6812795AD8/6F20C0F28B84AC5B3E9F27DD72202C7 (accessed April 4, 2013).

"Miscellaneous Telegrams." *Batavia Daily Morning News*, November 30, 1879. Old Fulton NY Post Cards. http://fultonhistory.com/ (accessed March 17, 2013).

"Newport Hard Hit by the Influenza." *Pawtucket Evening Times*, September 26, 1918. America's Historical Newspapers. NewsBank/American Antiquarian Society. 2004. http://docs.newsbank.com/s/HistArchive/ahnpdoc/EANX/120139C450835B20/6F20C08F28B84AC5B3E9F27DD72202C7 (accessed April 4, 2013).

"No Foul Play in Miss Mary Gleason's Death." *Boston Daily Globe*, January 27, 1925. ProQuest Historical Newspapers. NewsBank/American Antiquarian Society. 2004. http://pqasb.pqarchiver.com/boston/access/1879887472.html?FMT=AI&FMTS=CITE:AI&type=historic&date=Jan+27%2C+1925&author=&pub=Boston+Daily+Globe+%281923-1927%29&edition=&startpage=A4&desc=NO+FOUL+PLAY+IN+MISS+MARY+GLEASON%27S+DEATH (accessed February 20, 2013).

"Officers Probe Death of Girl." *Boston Daily Globe*, January 27, 1925. ProQuest Historical Newspapers. http://pqasb.pqarchiver.com/boston/access/1879883472.html?FMT=A1&FMTS=ABS:AI&type=h

istoric&date=Jan+27%2C+1925&author=&pub=Boston+Daily+Globe+%281923-1927%29&edition=&startpage=1&desc=OFFICERS+PROBE+DEATH+OF+GIRL (accessed February 20, 2013).

"Officials Cast Doubt on Confession of Murder." *Boston Daily Globe*, January 29, 1925. ProQuest Historical Newspapers. http://pqasb.pqarchiver.com/boston/access/1879901072.html?FMT=AI&FMTS=ABS:AI&type=historic&date=Jan+29%2C+1925&author=&pub=Boston+Daily+Globe+%281923-1927%29&edition=&startpage=A1&desc=OFFICIALS+CAST+DOUBT+ON+CONFESSION+OF+MURDER (accessed February 20, 2013).

"Official Weather: 02840." WeatherSource. http://weathersource.com/account/official-weather?location=02840&start-date=01%2F19%2F1925&end-date=01%2F19%2F1925&subscription-demo=1&sid=hqv3l7q19apkh3119f0c6pn3a5&search=1&station-id=19370&latitude=41.4755&longitude=-71.3095 (accessed August 1, 2012).

"Pardon." *Providence Gazette*, November 30, 1820. America's Historical Newspapers. NewsBank/American Antiquarian Society. 2004. http://docs.newsbank.com/s/HistArchive/ahnpdoc/EANX/1056BA09352E18FC/6F20C08F28B84AC5B3E9F27DD72202C7 (accessed April 4, 2013).

"Pardon." *Rhode-Island American*, December 1, 1820. America's Historical Newspapers. NewsBank/American Antiquarian Society. 2004. http://docs.newsbank.com/s/HistArchive/ahnpdoc/EANX/10E697F0F28E1F98/6F20C08F28B84AC5B3E9F27DD72202C7 (accessed April 4, 2013).

"Private J.A. Yeager Commits Suicide." *Pawtucket Evening Times*, August 24, 1901. America's Historical Newspapers. NewsBank/American Antiquarian Society. 2004. http://docs.newsbank.com/s/HistArchive/ahnpdoc/EANX/11F96A33D2DB9B30/6F20C08F28B84AC5B3E9F27DD72202C7 (accessed February 19, 2013).

"Register of Death of Regular Army, 1879 (Jul)–1880 (Jul)," 124–25. *U.S. Register of Deaths in the Regular Army, 1870–1889 Record for Franz Koppe*, National Archives. Ancestry.com. http://search.ancestry.com (accessed April 28, 2013).

"Soldier at Newport Says He Killed Woman." *New York Times*. January 30, 1925. ProQuest Historical Newspapers. http://search.proquest.com/docview/103554119/13DDFB083814BAD2D38/2?accountid=11087 (accessed March 17, 2013).

"The Soldier Murder." *National Police Gazette*. December 20, 1879. Old Fulton NY Post Cards. http://fultonhistory.com (accessed March 17, 2013).

"Special Hospitals Are Urged at Once." *Pawtucket Evening Times*, September 26, 1918. America's Historical Newspapers. NewsBank/American Antiquarian Society. 2004. http://docs.newsbank.com/s/HistArchive/ahnpdoc/EANX/120139C4DD009B38/6F20C08F28B84AC5B3E9F27DD72202C7 (accessed April 4, 2013).

"St. Mary's Church." Discover Beautiful Rhode Island. Rhode Island Tourism Division. 2013. http://www.visitrhodeisland.com/what-to-see/museums/1243/st-marys-church/ (accessed March 31, 2013).

"St. Mary's Church." St. Mary's Church. 2012. http://stmarynewport.org/history (accessed March 30, 2013).

"Tells of Vaccine to Stop Influenza." *Pawtucket Evening Times*, October 2, 1918. America's Historical Newspapers. NewsBank/American Antiquarian Society. 2004. http://docs.newsbank.com/s/HistArchive/ahnpdoc/EANX/120139D18AC0FDA0/6F20C08F28B84AC5B3E9F27DD72202C7 (accessed April 19, 2013).

"Terrible Explosion at Newport." *Boston Evening Transcript*, August 30, 1881. Google News. http://news.google.com/newspapers?id=bUJfAAAAIBAJ&sjid=iVQNAAAAIBAJ&pg=6676%2 (accessed April 4, 2013).

Titus, Daniel P., and Gerald Foley. "Preservation Plan for the Military Cemetery at Fort Adams." *Faculty and Staff—Articles & Papers*, no. 30 (2001). http://digitalcommons.salve.edu/fac_staff_pub/30 (accessed March 4, 2013).

"Touro Synagogue." Touro Synagogue National Historic Site. 2008–2012. http://tourosynagogue.org/index.php/history-learning/synagogue-history (accessed March 30, 2013).

United States v. Cornell. Case #14,867, Circuit Court, D. Rhode Island. 1819. YesWeScan: The Federal Cases. https://law.resource.org/pub/us/case/reporter/Hein/0025.f.cas/0025.f.cas.0646.3.pdf (accessed March 16, 2013).

"U.S. Army, Register of Enlistments, 1798–1914 for Richard Geary." *Register of Enlistments, United States Army*. 1911, 1914. National Archives. Ancestry.com. http://interactive.ancestry.com.

"U.S. City Directories, 1821–1989 for Richard Geary." *Newport Directory for the Year Ending July 1919*. National Archives. Ancestry.com. http://interactive.ancestry.com/ (accessed April 27, 2013).

"U.S. City Directories, 1821–1989 for Richard Sergeant Fort Adams Geary." *Newport Directory for the Year Ending 1915*. National Archives. Ancestry.com. http://interactive.ancestry.com/ (accessed April 27, 2013).

"U.S. Civil War Pension Index: General Index to Pension Files, 1861–1934 for Nelson Henry." National Archives. Ancestry.com. http://interactive.ancestry.com/ (accessed April 22, 2013).

"U.S. Military Burial Registers, 1768–1921 for Franz Koppe." *Record Book of Interments in the Post Cemetery at Fort Adams.* National Archives. Ancestry.com. http://interactive.ancestry.com/ (accessed April 22, 2013).

"Walter K. Wilbraham." American Battle Monuments Commission. www.dvrbs.com/Monuments/Collingswood/CollsWW2-WalterKWilbraham.htm (accessed April 20, 2013).

"Walter K. Wilbraham." Military Times Hall of Valor. Gannett. 2013. projects.militarytimes.com/citations-medals-awards/recipient.php?recipientid=114335 (accessed April 20, 2013).

"Why Blew the Stables Up?" *Pawtucket Evening Times,* December 21, 1898. America's Historical Newspapers. NewsBank/American Antiquarian Society. 2004. http://docs/newsbank.com/s/HistArchive/ahnpdoc/EANX/11F72C312BF9FAF8/6F20C08F28B84AC5B3E9F27DD72202C7 (accessed April 4, 2013).

(William Cornell: execution on schedule.) *Providence Gazette*, November 27, 1820. America's Historical Newspapers. NewsBank/American Antiquarian Society. 2004. http://docs.newsbank.com/s/HistArchive.ahnpdoc/EANX/1056BA07F438B059/6F20C08F28B84AC5B3E9F27DD72202C7 (accessed April 4, 2013).

(William Cornell found guilty at trial.) *Rhode-Island American*, November 23, 1819. America's Historical Newspapers. NewsBank/American Antiquarian Society. 2004. http://docs.newsbank.com/s/HistArchive/ahnpdoc/EANX/10E696DA6D3B2D88/6F20C08F28B84AC5B3E9F27DD72202C7 (accessed April 4, 2013).

(William Cornell granted sixty-day stay of execution.) *Rhode-Island Republican*, September 20, 1820. America's Historical Newspapers. NewsBank/American Antiquarian Society. 2004. http://docs.newsbank.com/s/HistArchive.ahnpdoc/EANX/10E69F4E6ABCAC80/6F20C08F28B84AC5B3E9F27DD72202C7 (accessed April 4, 2013).

(William Cornell kills William Kane at Fort Adams.) *Providence Gazette*. July 10, 1819. America's Historical Newspapers. NewsBank/American Antiquarian Society. 2004. http://docs.newsbank.com/s/HistArchive/ahnpdoc/EANX/1056B961F485DC44/6F20C08F28B84AC5B3E9F27DD72202C7 (accessed April 4, 2013).

(William Cornell kills William Kane at Fort Adams.) *Providence Patriot*, July 10, 1819. America's Historical Newspapers. NewsBank/American Antiquarian Society. 2004. http://docs.newsbank.com/s/HistArchive/ahnpdoc/EANX/10AE3B7B978D9E08/6F20C08F28B84AC5B3E9F27DD72202C7 (accessed April 4, 2013).

(William Cornell kills William Kane at Fort Adams.) *Rhode-Island American*, July 9, 1819. America's Historical Newspapers. NewsBank/American Antiquarian Society. 2004. http://docs.newsbank.com/s/HistArchive/ahnpdoc/EANX/10E696779C2CFB70/6F20C08F28B84AC5B3E9F27DD72202C7 (accessed April 4, 2013).

(William Cornell kills William Kane at Fort Adams.) *Rhode-Island Republican*, July 7, 1819. America's Historical Newspapers. NewsBank/American Antiquarian Society. 2004. http://docs/newsbank.com/s/

HistArchive/ahnpdoc/EANX/10E69EB62B2BD970/6F20C08F28B84AC5B3E9F27DD72202C7 (accessed April 4, 2013).

(William Cornell: mother travels to Washington.) *Providence Patriot*, June 28, 1820. America's Historical Newspapers. NewsBank/American Antiquarian Society. 2004. http://docs.newsbank.com/s/HistArchive/ahnpdoc/EANX/10AE3CC95987D3E0/6F20C08F28B84AC5B3E9F27DD72202C7 (accessed April 4, 2013).

Index

B

Bernard, Simon 57
Boardman, Jim 93
Borden, Lizzie Andrew 18
Bradford. *See* Spalding, Lyman G.
Brown, John. *See* Koppe, Franz
Butler, John 60
  ghost of 98
Butler, William H. 65
  remains discovered 67

C

Caldwell, A.G. *See* Spalding, Lyman G.
Cazy, John 62
cemetery, Fort Adams 45, 51, 67
  percentages for women and children burials 35
Cemetery, Jewish 67
Cemetery, St. Columba's 85
children, ghosts of 98
Cook, John 45
Cordy, George C. 85
Cornell, Innocent 18
Cornell, Rebecca 17
Cornell, Sarah 18
Cornell, Thomas 17
Cornell, William G. 14
Costello, Abillio 69
countermines. *See* tunnels

D

Davis, Harry C. 50
d'Estaing, Comte 41
Drake, George F. 18

E

Edes, Benjamin L. 53
1812, War of 43

F

fire (1898) 65
fishing boat accident, 1827 44
Fitch, Seeley J. 51
Florio, Maggie 96
Ford, Walter L. 50
Fortifications Board 43

G

Geary baby 79
  burial at Fort Adams cemetery 79
Geary, Delia Theresa 79
Gleason, Mary 82
Goat Island. *See* torpedo station
Goetzinger, Bill 94
Gorman, Peter 30
Gragg, Oliver, Jr. 44

H

Halsey, James 63
Hammond, J.F. *See* Koppe, Franz
Harris, Harry I. 65
  remains discovered 66
Hathaway, William H. 50
Henderson, George P. 82
Henry, Ellen
  community relief efforts 37
  pension granted 37
  shot 36
Henry, Nelson 36
Holland, William 51
Howard 19

I

influenza, 1918
  among the navy 73, 75
  at Fort Adams 75, 77
  called "Spanish Influenza" 73
  closure of public places 76
  closure of public schools 76
  Fort Adams death toll 79
  marking of affected homes 77
  national death toll 79
  peak reached in Newport 77
  preventative recommendations 74
  Rhode Island death toll 79
  vaccine 74, 79
Irish, Fort Adams laborers 60

J

Jones, James M. 29

K

Kane, William 14
  ghost of 98
Kennedy, John F.
  President 39
Kennedy, Patrick 61
Kerrigan. *See* Howard
Koppe, Franz 21
Kotlen, Lisa 91
Kull, Frederick W. 65
  remains discovered 66

L

Lafayette, Marquisde 41
Lajoie, Ephraim 65
Lane. *See* Koppe, Franz
Langdon, Timothy R. 30
Lewis, Ida 49
Lourie, H.E. *See* Drake, George F.

M

Manney, Henry L. *See* Spalding, Lyman G.
Mayo, Private 65
Moulton, Thomas 50

N

Nicholson, William 21
  arrested for murder of Franz Koppe 26
  released 28

O

overnight barracks 92

Q

Quin, Michael 62

R

Revolutionary War 13
Rhode Island, Battle of 42
Rice, Peter 46

S

Selfridge. *See* Spalding, Lyman G.
Sheehan, William 50
Slack, W.H. *See* Spalding, Lyman G.
Spalding, Lyman G. 53
  ghost of 98
St. Mary's 60

T

Newport Artillery Company, The 41
Rhode Island Paranormal Research Group, The (TRIPRG) 94, 96, 97, 98, 100
torpedo station 53
Totten, Joseph G. 57
Touro Synagogue 67, 110
Tousard, Louis 13
Tracy, John 61
  ghost of 98
tunnels 58

W

Walker, Robert 30
Wilbraham, Walter K.
  car crash 71
  dies at fort hospital 71
  performs rescue at sea 70

Y

Yeager, John A. 30

About the Author

Kathleen Troost-Cramer grew up in Portsmouth, Rhode Island, and developed a fascination with local history at an early age. This interest led to a twenty-four-season career as a tour guide at various locations, including the Newport mansions, the Lizzie Borden Bed & Breakfast/Museum in Fall River and Fort Adams, where Kathleen developed the original Halloween attraction Fortress of Nightmares. Kathleen is currently pursuing a ThD in biblical studies from Boston University School of Theology. *True Tales* is her first published work. Visit Kathleen's website at ktroostc.wix.com/books.

Visit us at
www.historypress.net

This title is also available as an e-book